MW01229101

Published by:
Breton Bay
Dalton House
60 Windsor Avenue
London
SW19 2RR
United Kingdom

ISBN 978-0-9558347-1-4

1. TRAVEL / General
2. TRAVEL / Europe / France
3. TRAVEL / Europe / France / Paris
4. TRAVEL / Europe / General

Copyediting: Erin Hartshorn, Kanittha Kantree
Interior & Cover Design: Within Design Co., Ltd.
Cover Image: Fotosearch
Other Images: Shutterstock
www.sensualparis.com
info@sensualparis.com

SENSUAL PARIS

A Guide to Sex, Seduction & Romance in the Sublime City of Light

By

Jonathan LeBlanc Roberts

BRETON BAY

About the Author

Jonathan LeBlanc Roberts served as Executive Director of the Hollywood-Los Angeles Film Commission where he managed motion picture production and served as liaison to the major studios and independent production companies. He was also instrumental in planning dozens of annual entertainment industry events such as the Academy Awards and Grammy Awards. After relocating to France, he worked as an executive at a Paris-based film marketing company and entertainment news producer while covering international film festivals such as Cannes, Sundance, Berlin, Venice and Toronto. His secondary interest and studies in anthropology account for his quirky fascination with Franco-American/Anglo cultural differences. A Canadian-American, he has resided abroad for the past decade, most of that time in Paris.

How to Submit Corrections, Updates and Ideas to the Editor

Readers:

Interested readers are invited to email the editor with pertinent information, tips, ideas, or suggestions for future editions (A revised, updated SENSUAL PARIS Guide will be published annually). Contact: ideas@sensualparis.com.

Business Owners & Managers

Every effort has been made to provide current and accurate information for all of the venues, commercial establishments and attractions listed. Business owners and managers may submit changes, updates, and corrections to the editor to be included in the annual updated edition. Contact: updates@sensualparis.com.

A Disclaimer

Acknowledgements

I want to thank Marie-Elizabeth Crochard for her generous advice and insight into all things French, and her husband, author Jean-Marie Fitère, for his guidance on the pleasures, joys and temptations of *La Vie Parisienne.*

For their assistance long ago, in facilitating my introduction to Parisian life and society, I am especially grateful to Edward Flaherty, Robert Price, Adrian Leeds and the late Mort Segal.

Arms of the City of Paris

Table of Contents

About the Author 6

Acknowledgements 7

Chapter One: The Parisian Life - *La Vie Parisienne* 11

The French Culture 11
The Sublime City 11
Seduction & Romance in the French Historical Context 12
Looking at the French Stereotype 15

Chapter Two: Seduction French Style (à la Française) 17

Sexual Mystique of the Modern French Female 18
The French Male - By Means of Flattery, Wit & Charm 20
A Few Lessons in Seduction: 21
A Primer on Cross-Cultural Seduction for the Anglo or American Man 21
A Primer on Cross-Cultural Seduction for the Anglo or American Woman 24
The Mystique of Mystique 26
Etiquette, Behavior and Customs: 27
Paris Rendezvous on the Web 29

Chapter Three: French Attitudes – Sex & Sexuality 31

The French are Different than Us 32
The Etiquette of Infidelity 34
Etiquette of Infidelity—France 36
The Etiquette of Infidelity—America 37
Repercussions 38
Politics without the Sex Scandal 39

Chapter Four: Shopping - the Chic & Sexy Woman 41

Fine French Lingerie – The Power to Seduce 42
Boutiques - Shopping for the Best Lingerie 45
Lingerie in the Department Stores *(Les Grandes Magasins)* 46
A Primer for Men – How to Purchase the Perfect Lingerie for your Wife, Girlfriend, or Mistress 47
The "Last Word" on Lingerie 48
Zen of the High Heel 49
The Debut of the High Heel Shoe 50
Sexy Shoes & Boots *(Chaussures & Bottes)* 50
Designer Sex Boutiques for the Ladies *(Les Sex Toys)* 52

Chapter Five: Hotels - Sensual & Romantic 55

Recommended Hotels for Lovers 56

Chapter Six: Restaurants – Passionate Epicurean Pleasures 63

Recommended Restaurants for Lovers 64
Cafés – Life in the Slow Lane 72

Chapter Seven: The Exuberant Parisian Nightlife **77**
Bars & Lounges 78
Dance Clubs 82
Uber-Chic Clubs - Clubbing with Attitude 85
VIP Soirées 86
Jazz Clubs 87
Erotic Cabarets & Nightclubs 89
Intimate Cabarets 90

Chapter Eight: The Paris Day Spa – Indulgent Care of the Body **91**

Chapter Nine: Eclectic Adventures, Diversions & Frivolous Amusements **97**
Romantic Cinema 100
French School of Seduction *(Ecole Française de Séduction)* 101
Small but very Memorable Museums 103
Montmartre Museum of Erotic Art *(Musée de l'Erotisme)* 104
Jacquemart André Museum *(Musee Jacquemart André)* 104
Rodin Museum *(Musée Rodin)* 104
Museum of the Romantic Life *(Musée de la Vie Romantique)* 105
Le Cordon Bleu Paris 105
Rendezvous at Parc de Bagatelle 106
Sunday Night Dinner in Paris 107
Erotic Bookstores *(Libraries Érotique)* 108
Galleries - Erotica & Collectibles 109

Chapter Ten: Paris as Therapy **111**
A Sojourn in Paris 112
The Art of Living *(Art de Vivre)* 114

Chapter Eleven: Erotic Clubbing **115**
Paris Libertine Clubs 116
The Private Club *(Club Privé)* 117
Who attends the Clubs? 117
I Like to Watch 118
Club Entrance Policies & Etiquette 118
Special Theme Evenings *(Soirées a Theme)* 119
Erotic Entertainment 124
The "New Civilized" Strip Tease Clubs 124
Strip Clubs for Ladies Only - Girls want to have Fun 125

Chapter Twelve: Gay & Lesbian Paris **127**
Bars & Cafés 128

Chapter Thirteen: Dangerous Liaisons— Fantasy, Fetish & Fashion **131**
Missing Your Moment in History 132
Fetish Culture & Eroticism from Fashion to Hollywood 134

Chapter Fourteen: Venal Pleasures **139**
Eighteenth Century Bacchanalia 140
La Belle Époque 142
The Grand Bordellos *(Maisons Closes)* 142

Chapter Fifteen: Sexy French Glossary & Phrase Book **147**
Flirtation 150
Sex Play 152
Salacious Slang 155
Withering Insults 156

Chapter One:
The Parisian Life–La Vie Parisienne

1

Chapter One:

"Give me chastity
and self-restraint,
but do not give it yet!"

~ Saint Augustine ~

Paris is often celebrated as the most seductive city in the world, synonymous with pleasure, passion and romance. It is a fanciful and beguiling oasis of art, culture, stunningly harmonious architecture and cosmopolitan sophistication. A feast for the senses, the city is effervescent with the enchantment of fine cuisine, wine and haute couture, all exquisitely embellished by the Parisian's none-too-subtle proclivity for sensual decadence. This great capital city provides the adventuresome the prospect of discovering countless hidden pleasures limited only by the imagination.

The French Culture... What does it mean to be French? It means that one places a high value on family, culture, and the vital pleasures. There is a profound commitment to a style of life that places greater emphasis on tradition, a slower pace, and a certain grander notion of existence.

In France one is more likely to be judged on his or her intellect and knowledge of culture and history, than on the size of his home, the value of his bank account or the automobile he drives. He should speak the language flawlessly and possess that natural—*je ne sais quois*. He should be comfortable in his own skin regardless of his station in life, his social class or his economic and professional achievements.

The Sublime City... Parisians enjoy their global reputation for heightened sensuality and occasional sexual excess. This small 38 square mile (98 sq km) city offers abundant and unsuspected pleasures at every turn.

Paris is a city built for walking and for *lounging about*—wasting time—ensconced in the café, watching the world go by—strolling through the Luxembourg Gardens or the Tuileries. To be candid, it is much more difficult lounging about in New York, London or Tokyo because most of your peers reckon that you should be busy working. But in France, leisure remains an indispensable part of life, and as every Parisian understands, it is an essential ingredient in the pursuit of pleasure. The intoxicating mix of architecture, sumptuous gardens and ancient bridges over the Seine are all part of the charm that intensely arouses the passion of visitors and residents alike.

Thus, Paris remains a bright sensual lamp that illuminates the rest of the world and draws the world's attention onto itself. Epicureans, intellectuals and libertines seem to inevitably make their sojourn to Paris like true believers performing their pilgrimage to a sacred shrine. Over many centuries, writers, philosophers, artists, poets and revolutionaries have gathered here to bask in the warmth of its enlightened society and liberal traditions.

Seduction & Romance in the French Historical Context... It is important to appreciate that when we speak of "seduction," we are speaking in the broader French and original Latin sense of the term. In English, seduction is most often utilized as a sexual term and not infrequently one with the negative connotation of the deceiver or philanderer. But in French, *séduction* is closer to a social act of playful charm, used at times, but not always, in a romantic or sexual context.

The modern French notion of love, romance and seduction first emerged in the twelfth and thirteenth centuries with the troubadours. These romantic storytellers and songwriters entertained at the royal courts of Aquitaine, Toulouse and Provence in the South of France. Through their songs, the troubadours offered an innovative perspective on the traditional view of love and marriage. Instead of arranged marriages for the purpose of consolidating properties through shrewd family alliances, they sang of passion and idealized *romantic love*. Over time, elaborate courtship rituals evolved encompassing this fundamental social concept. These rituals spread throughout France and most of the Western world by means of French romantic literature and poetry.

This is an example of a troubadour song written in AD 1200 by *Cindessa de Dia* (The Countess of Die), a lady troubadour from the Languedoc region.

I Was Plunged Into Deep Distress

I was plunged into deep distress / by a knight who wooed me,

and I wish to confess for all time / how passionately I loved him;

Now I feel myself betrayed / for I did not tell him of my love.

Therefore I suffer great distress / in bed and when I am fully dressed.

Would that my knight might one night / lie naked in my arms and find myself in ecstasy / with me as his pillow.

For I am more in love with him / than Floris was with Blanchfleur.

To him I give my heart and love / my reason, eyes and life.

Handsome friend, tender and good / when will you be mine?

Oh, to spend with you but one night / to impart the kiss of love!

Know that with passion I cherish / the hope of you in my husband's place, as soon as you have sworn to me / that you will fulfill my every wish. (www.languedoc-france.info - June 2007)

While the preeminent hero in most ancient cultures is the larger-than-life warrior or conqueror, the enduring role model of the French is the tenacious lover pursuing his or her quest with intense devotion and unbridled passion. French history and literature are heavily laden with heroes and heroines fiercely, helplessly, and deeply in love. For the French, sexual desire is the source of the feelings of love. In *Discourse on the Passion of Love*, Pascal says, "passion cannot be beautiful without excess. When one does not love too much, one does not love enough."

Perhaps there is no better example in all of French literature than *Cyrano de Bergerac,* the larger than life character in the immortal play by Edmond Rostand in which chivalry, wit and bravery are forever captured in a timeless spirit of romance. Set in Louis XIII's reign, it is the compelling drama of one of the best swordsmen in France, gallant soldier, brilliant wit and tragic poet-lover, blessed with an extraordinarily large nose. Cyrano is a deeply passionate and articulate man who represents purity of purpose and unyielding honor.

In the early eighteenth century, Pierre Carlet de Chamblain de Marivaux was responsible for further defining French courtship rules among the aristocratic elite.

"Marivaux (1688–1763), the French: playwright was known for his mastery of the *politesses amoureuses,* or the polite expressions of the human heart in love. In Marivaux's world, the highly ordered French 18th century society, it was incumbent on prospective lovers to speak with delicacy, to master the arts of concealment and disclosure of the emotions, and above all to be able to have maximum capacity to influence the heart of another. Conversation was not just a means of communication, but a fine instrument for pleasures of the mind as well as for the purpose of seduction.

In its most essential form, *marivaudage* aims at coaxing love from the beloved by means of stratagems, then it also captures one of the essential contradictions of Paris - of the light and shadow sides of the city that is romantic and enchanted, but also somehow calculating and remorseless. Everyone is or wants to be in love or loved, everyone understands the Rules of the Game and yet almost all rules can be broken in the pursuit of *l'amour.*

In Marivaux's view, the pursuit was governed by a delicate interplay of flirtation and elegantly articulated words of seduction. In this milieu, *l'amour* is as much defined by the chase as by the conquest.

In any case, while happiness and fulfillment are possible outcomes, they are neither the goal nor the ideal of this view of love. Happiness and fulfillment were overlaid as ideals upon this vision by the *bourgeoisie*, who needed to justify marriage economically, and to rationalize their guilt about arranged marriage. It was ok to throw one's daughter into unpredictability and peril, even if the husband seemed boorish, because love leads to happiness, and love buttressed by money virtually assures it. To the degree that we, in our contemporary world, have laundered our passion by belief in love as the passport to happiness—bad outcomes being accidents or quirks of fate, somewhat like airplane disasters—it is possible that we have devolved, gone backwards from a more advanced view of passion." (From Studios St-Sulpice)

Looking at the French Stereotype... In discussing the characteristics of a national culture, we do not suggest that every person in the nation exhibits all of the assigned characteristics. So in describing a national culture, we refer to the recognized common elements within a nation; but we are not describing individuals. (Hofstede)

A nuanced assessment of the French might be as follows: The French are Latin in their behavior—very much influenced by early Roman and Mediterranean culture; they have a chivalrous temperament; are very idealistic; quick to support a cause; adventurous; very family oriented; intensely demonstrative; extremely individualistic; quick-tempered; notably class conscious (preoccupied with rank, status and formality); inventive; exceedingly mindful of history; constantly inclined to try to beat the system; bold in character; commonsensical; intensely private; followers of fashion; deeply suspicious; quick-witted and capable of deflating another's ego with a mere word or gesture; highly analytical and logical to a fault. The French strive to create harmony and beauty in their environment; they are strikingly civilized; cynical and come armed with a mocking sense of humor. They maintain traditional values; are acutely focused on form and style; are tactful; diplomatic; gloriously food obsessed and extraordinarily precise in their language.

And yes, they are passionate. Their sensuality is reflected in every aspect of their daily lives from their ribald sense of humor, to their risqué advertising, to their endless fascination with the rituals of seduction.

Sociologists report that they are more adventurous than most in the fulfillment of their sexual fantasies. They tend to be more accepting of exotic forms of pleasure, and as long as one is a willing participant, almost anything goes. The French freely admit to having an obsession with sex but it is truly an adult obsession.

Chapter Two:
Seduction French Style (à la Française)

Chapter Two:

"The desire of the man is for the woman, but the desire of the woman is for the desire of the man."

~ Germaine de Stael,
French woman of letters
1766–1817 ~

Americans and Anglos seeking romance in Paris may find pleasure or peril depending upon how successfully they contend with the contrasting cultural and behavioral codes. A cross-cultural relationship tempered with good communication and mutual understanding might be an exciting prospect.

In some respects dating in France is like turning the clock back to a more traditional era before the inexorable creep of political correctness (in North America and the UK) began to confuse and often hinder the male-female relationship.

In France the natural state of the gender dynamic is fully intact and no one wants to see that change, even French feminists. French women have embraced feminism without sacrificing their femininity.

Indeed, the male - female rules of engagement appear to have shifted in intriguing ways for modern French women. They are taking the initiative, and there has been a marked increase in their sexual assertiveness. Women demand pleasure and if they cannot find it with their husband or boyfriend they will seek it elsewhere.

"We want to keep the freedom to be seduced—and to seduce," wrote feminist philosopher Sylviane Agacinski, wife of former French Prime Minister Lionel Jospin, in her 1998 book, *Sexual Politics.* "[T]here will be no war of the sexes in France perhaps because here we like friendship and love, seduction and even licentiousness *(libertinage)* too much."

Sexual Mystique of the Modern French Female...

Through two thousand years of history, French women have leveraged their resourcefulness and audacious spirit to achieve their objectives, wielding political influence over kings, presidents and generations of powerful men. During the celebrated Golden Age of Salons (seventeenth and eighteenth centuries), French women established their dominion over the intellectual realm where artistic, social, literary and philosophical trends were determined.

Powerful women served as both belligerents and intellectual provocateurs during the turbulent rebellion against the French monarchy. One of most enduring icons of the Republic is the heroic figure of "Liberty," her insurgent breasts exposed; lifting the national flag in one hand, brandishing a musket in the other as she fearlessly storms the barricades. This celebrated, allegorical painting by Eugène Delacroix honors the role of women in the revolutions of 1789 and 1830.

Modern French women exhibit a high degree of poise and personal self-confidence that has come from centuries of getting their way in their own inherent fashion. American Author Edith Wharton who spent thirty years in France says in *The French and Their Ways:* the French woman "is in nearly all respects, as different as possible from the average American woman. Is it because she dresses better, or knows more about cooking, or is more coquettish, or more feminine, or more emotional, or more immoral? The real reason is not nearly as flattering to our national vanity. It is simply that the French woman is more grown-up. Compared with the women of France the average American woman is still in kindergarten."

Helena Frith Powell, the bright and beautiful British author of *Two Lipsticks and a Lover,* and a host of other books about France says, "Whereas in England it is embarrassing to be intellectual, in France it is essential. And the extraordinary thing is French women see intellectual rigor almost as important as their beauty regime. It is not enough to look good to be seductive; you have to be cultured as well."

In the modern world the French woman has learned to strike a delicate balance retaining her feminine prerogatives while still demanding respect in the social and professional world. According to Debra Ollivier, author of *Entre Nous,* there is "less contradiction between being sexy and being a professional" in French society. It is socially acceptable for a woman to be ultra-feminine, to dress in a captivating style, and to appropriately exploit her feminine mystique.

"The 'quiet,' coded game of love is often baffling to us 'imprudently' direct Anglos, but it's partly what's kept French women in the sexiness hall of fame for centuries. Never mind haute couture or racy lingerie. French women are a bundle of alluring contradictions that seem to perfectly coexist, like the unlikely mélange of sweet and sour. They're often annoyingly coy and darkly wanton. Many of them are not great beauties and yet are gorgeously compelling in the way they reconcile their imperfections. They tend to be more concerned with experiencing pleasure than with being liked and far more passionate about having a life than making a living."

"There is so much pressure on American women to be happy. To sweep away all traces of loneliness, to forget who you are in your search for a lover or a spouse. In France young girls learn that happiness is elusive; they learn that happiness is less important than passion."

"We never confused the power of feminism with the power of femininity, the power of the femme. Being a grown-up to a French woman means being complete, with or without a man, but still being in love with love." (Debra Ollivier, *What French Girls Know,* Salon.com, 2004)

Critics rightly complain that French women have not broken through to positions at the very top tier of the political and corporate world, though significant gains have been made. Edith Cresson served as Prime Minister in the early 1990's and Segolene Royal was the Socialist candidate for President in 2007. The winner of that election, Nicolas Sarkozy appointed seven female ministers, the largest number ever in a French government.

The French Male - By Means of Flattery, Wit & Charm... In the never-ending Gallic cat-and-mouse game of seduction, the counterpoint to the ultra-feminine female is the charming French male who, in order to succeed must demonstrate that he knows how to properly court a woman. He must show that he is engaging, witty and well raised *(bien élevé).*

Flirting is considerably more than a simple act of lighthearted fun—it's a fundamental aspect of the human social order and a step in the indispensable reproductive process that assures the continuation of our species.

Anthropologists say that flirting exists in one form or another in every society around the world, yet in cultures that have developed an over-bearing sense of political correctness, the ability to flirt has markedly declined. There is fear that one may offend, that their attention may be misunderstood or worse that their efforts might be perceived as sexual harassment.

France is a Latin culture, and Latin males are more exuberant in these endeavors. They come up with some pretty outrageous lines, and women who come from a more restrained culture may see this as fairly aggressive behavior. But it is the way things are done. French men constantly hone their skills by flirting with grandmothers, librarians and the butcher's wife. They are doing what comes natural in their society. Most French women just laugh and ignore it if they feel the attention is overly persistent. They are very adroit at discouraging a man with a bit of cutting humor if necessary.

The French flirt incessantly. They are on automatic-pilot, barely able to turn it off. As the Vicomte de Valmont succinctly states in the novel and film *Dangerous Liaisons* "It's beyond my control." Yet flirtation is often just a good-natured, amusing game unrelated to sexual seduction. For both French men and women it serves as a basic and fundamental part of the social toolkit. Flattery, wit and charm are the necessary means to an end whether that end is getting the best table in a restaurant, tickets to a sold out concert, or a better break from the tax-collector.

All of this hyper-Gallic energy comes into sharp focus in the French capital, which exudes a level of amorous intrigue that does not exist elsewhere.

A Few Lessons in Seduction:
A Primer on Cross-cultural Seduction for the American or Anglo Man

Intellect... French women should first be seduced intellectually—entice her mind - her heart and all else will follow. By and large, Parisian women are well educated, articulate and well read, so make the most of your knowledge of history, art, culture and current events.

Profession... In France, unlike America and Britain, what you do for a living is not necessarily what defines you. Your professional accomplishments and responsibilities are often seen as less important than your cultural depth, and your sense of style. Therefore, avoid droning on about your business and professional life and focus on what you know and not what you do.

Flattery... Subtle compliments can be enchanting if properly chosen and deftly delivered. Simply telling a beautiful, well-dressed woman that she is beautiful or her outfit is attractive is uninspiring and she probably hears it all the time. Use some creativity and find a less obvious attribute to applaud. To hit the mark, compliments must sound genuine and spontaneous.

Focus... Ask about her interests and her lifestyle; however, in the beginning avoid asking about her family (a very private matter in France). Ask open-ended questions and listen intently, maintaining good eye contact. Our undivided attention is perhaps the most intoxicating and powerful gift we can bestow on a woman. Throughout history, the legendary seducers such as Prince Aly Khan, Porfirio Rubirosa, Jean-Paul Sartre and John F. Kennedy all had the capacity to make the object of their desire feel as if she were the only female in the room.

Charm... There is a wonderfully instructive episode in French history regarding the Duchesse de Longueville, who enjoyed the company of many male admirers at the royal court. One day a female friend asked her whether she preferred the company of the witty Duc de Montausier or the company of the dashing Chevalier de Chatillon. The Duchesse de Longueville sagely replied that when she dined with the Duc de Montausier she left the meal thinking that he was the most interesting person in all of France. However, when she dined with the Chevalier de Chatillon, she left feeling that 'she' was the most interesting person in all of France.

This is the very essence of charm and seduction. If you wish to successfully captivate the object of your desire the point is to make her feel that the earth and the planets rotate around her . . . not around you.

Money... Any discussion of personal income and the usual material status symbols is frowned upon in France. They have a curious but remarkably refreshing attitude about all matters related to money—they simply don't talk about it.

Drink... At least consider drinking in relative moderation. In France being visibly intoxicated in public is widely viewed as boorish. This may be challenging for the hard drinking Brits and Americans.

Humor... It is next to impossible to flirt and seduce successfully without humor and in surveys French women repeatedly say they consider a good sense of humor to be one of the most attractive characteristics they seek in a man. Self-effacing humor can be the most disarming.

Thank You... The French have an obsession with the written word. It is almost as if a thought or idea does not exist unless it is expressed in writing. So in a world of the ubiquitous mobile phone, SMS messaging and email, nothing is quite as intimate as a hand-written personal note sent the day after a particularly pleasurable rendezvous. If you were really smitten, say it with flowers. There is a flower shop on practically every corner in Paris because statistically the French bestow more flowers on loved ones than any other nation in Europe.

Dress Code... How to dress in Paris? It becomes more challenging to generalize about this all the time. During the day you can usually dress according to your own personal preferences with the exception of shorts, sweats and sneakers (called trainers in the UK). Parisians simply don't wear this attire unless they are working out at the gym. For the evening, dress more fashionably, especially if you are going to dinner at a better bistro, restaurant or upscale club. Obviously, "appropriate attire" varies greatly depending upon your age group, social circle and destination. In Paris the old adage still applies, *when in doubt wear black.*

Manners... French women expect their partner to have good table manners, and a reasonable knowledge of cuisine and wine.

Amour... Don't lose sight of the fact that you are in the most conducive city on the planet for romance, so exploit the numerous Parisian locales designed to create the mood for amour.

Passion... Despite their seductive reputation French women may not be quite as quick to jump in the sack as some may believe; nevertheless, they can be intensely spontaneous when they wish to be. Parisian women are ultra-urbane and don't play mind games, so if she is in an amorous frame of mind she may accept an invitation alone to your hotel or residence, or she may invite you alone to hers. In the French social context, this generally means that she is sexually available. That said, women can and do change their mind.

You will likely find that the Gallic female is remarkably verbal, direct and uninhibited in articulating her sexual desires and demands. As Balzac noted of Parisian women, "when they're truly in love they surrender themselves to their passions far more completely than most other women."

A Primer on Cross-cultural Seduction for the American or Anglo Woman

Successful cross-cultural dating for the English speaking woman can be enhanced by striking just the right balance—exploiting your own appealing cultural characteristics while simultaneously adopting some of the coquettish traits practiced to such good effect by French women. A few suggestions for those wishing to woo the French male:

Intellect... The French are highly analytical and thrive on debate, so be lively, engaging and flaunt your rhetorical skills. French men believe that wit and a keen intellect are provocative and sexy. Says author Helena Frith Powell, "In France it doesn't seem possible to talk, write or have sex just for the sake of it. There always has to be an intellectual element to it. Maybe this is because French women argue seduction has almost as much to do with the mind as it does their looks; as much to do with her ability to quote Baudelaire as with her bra. She sees intelligence and knowledge as another accessory to complete her look and image." (Helena Frith Powell, *Two Lipsticks and a Lover,* 2006).

Profession... For Americans and Anglos the first question asked is "What do you do for a living?" Based on the response, a mental profile is formed regarding the individual's place in society. In France, your occupation is not what defines you, rather, what you know, your cultural depth, and your sense of style is what characterizes you as an individual. It is a different way of looking at the world. Also, in the early stages of a dating relationship avoid asking about his family (a very private matter in France).

Language... Parisian men are truly fascinated by women from other cultures and he will likely find your accent charming. If you speak a bit of French, this is your chance to try it out.

Dress Code... Dress smart with a chic, understated style. If you want to follow French fashion, wear fitted attire that accentuates your figure and wear heels. For the evening, dress more fashionably if you are going to dinner at a nice bistro, restaurant or upscale club. It is useful to remember author Françoise Sagan's sage advice "A dress makes no sense unless it inspires men to want to take it off you." Parisians simply don't wear shorts, sweats or sneakers out and about as they are seen as attire appropriate for working out at the gym. Obviously, "appropriate attire" varies greatly depending upon your age group, social circle and destination.

Coquetry... A quintessential facet of coquetry is, in the same moment to be both ingratiating and regally self-assured. The magical elixir of these seemingly opposing characteristics is intoxicating to men. So, precisely what does a French man respond to? Well, this is not complicated. He responds to virtually the same approach every other male on the planet responds to—discreet charm, flattery, and a subtle appreciation of his admirable qualities and manhood.

Lingerie... Wear your most extravagant set of matching lingerie. It will make you feel ultra-feminine and if you become intimate you will be exquisitely prepared to bewitch your partner.

Makeup... No one has ever improved upon Yves Saint Laurent's legendary advice "The most beautiful makeup for a woman is passion. But cosmetics are easier to buy."

Money... The old joke in Paris is that Americans *always* talk about money and the French *always* talk about sex. Americans and Anglos may be awkward frankly discussing sex, while the French are always *awkward* discussing any issue related to money (income, wealth, possesions). Despite these amusing national quirks, successful cross-cultural relationships develop everyday.

Humor... Both French men and women are grown-up adults, and sexual humor, some fairly explicit, is never viewed as "politically incorrect."

Perfume... Select your own special fragrance at the local perfume boutique. Where to apply your perfume, you ask? "Wherever you want to be kissed," advised fashion great Coco Chanel.

Passion... Cross-cultural dating always has the potential to create social misunderstandings. A foreign female, whether she is in an amorous frame of mind or not, should be *completely* aware that if she invites a man *alone* to her hotel or residence or goes *alone* to his, then within the French social context, she has indicated that she is sexually available.

Relationships... After dating for a relatively brief period of time American women often want to define where the relationship stands—*Honey, can we talk about us?* You are ill advised to pursue this approach in France. Both men and women are comfortable in letting matters remain intangible for quite some time without discussing the future or spelling out the parameters of the relationship. So resist the urge.

The Mystique of Mystique... "There is a culture in France of the *'non-dit,'* the not-spoken. What you don't say in France is as important as what is said. There are boundaries in language that create tensions. Even sexual tensions. The simple act of saying 'tu' or 'vous' is a boundary that invites intimacy or precludes it. We learn that we have more power when we keep things to ourselves than when we give things away. We learn that the art of seduction is based on innuendo and silences." (Debra Ollivier, *What French Girls Know,* Salon.com, 2004).

American and British women, open and affable by nature, tend to be more forthright, promptly laying their cards on the table, figuratively speaking. But there is magic and mystique to be found in the female who remains a bit of an enigma. The advantage of cultivating this aura of mystery in romantic relationships, particularly in the early stages, is that the imagination of the other is allowed to work overtime. This idealization does not occur if we know too much about the other person. An alternating sense of interest and detachment will often produce a sense of fascination and desire.

Obviously this approach is equally effective for men as for women. If you have qualms about utilizing craft and artifice in the pursuit of love, know that for centuries the French have justified most anything to win at love. Their view is that as you enjoy the blissful rewards of *amour,* pedestrian reality will return soon enough so revel in passion while you can.

"Civility is a desire to receive civility, and to be thought polite."

~ François, duc de La Rochefoucauld (1613–1680) ~

Etiquette, Behavior and Customs:

Greetings... Greetings in this polite society are somewhat formal. You should greet people in a very specific fashion—"Bonjour, monsieur" or "madame." It is considered good manners when entering a shop or boutique to say hello to the proprietor and goodbye when you leave. This initial greeting will set the proper tone and establish the basis for a positive experience. Failure to follow this small courtesy can be seen as rude and may result in a more chilly reception or even a lack of prompt service. While it may appear to be an odd notion to Anglos, French people see a shop or boutique as an extension of their home. See Chapter 15 - *Sexy French Glossary and Phrasebook* for a full range of greetings.

The Kiss *(La Bise)*... The exchange of a light kiss on each cheek is the familiar social greeting between French family, friends and acquaintances. In Paris, two kisses are customary starting, with right cheek to right cheek, then left to left. Because it is necessary to kiss everyone on arrival and departure, Americans and Anglos often look on with amusement when in a restaurant a French person joins or leaves a party of eight. The result is a great deal of kissing.

If you venture out into the far reaches of France the number of kisses becomes more complicated: In the Southeast of the country it is three; in the Southwest & Northeast it is two; in the West it is one; and in the Northwest it is four. Is that clear?

The Enigmatic French Smile... It is a characteristic of French social behaviour not to smile at strangers on the street (or generally in public). The French traditionally maintain a restrained public persona and keep the warmer side of their personality for their friends and family. This seemingly minor difference in their public demeanor is the cause of much cross-cultural confusion and misunderstanding. It is frequently misinterpreted by visiting foreigners as rudeness or arrogance. But the smiles readily appear when the French respond to humor or when they are flirtatious.

Americans are known to be casual and outgoing, and they expect to be able to easily approach strangers. While a bit more reserved than Americans, the British are still poles apart from the French. So how does one bridge the divide? It takes more of a committment to grasp the Gallic way of things but the rewards are significant.

It's in the Eyes... While you may not make headway on the street or in the Métro with your smile, you *can* flirt with your eyes. It is a much more subtle art. You simply smile with your eyes rather than your mouth. It is also more socially acceptable in France to directly stare at another individual. French women are accustomed to being stared at and admired by men so they generally welcome the attention. Afterall, in flaunting their feminity they are not exactly surprised or offended when it engenders a response. "Listen to what she says with her eyes" Victor Hugo.

Dining & Table Manners... Always make dining reservations, even at a small neighbourhood bistro. Many Parisian restaurants have a limited number of tables and often have a single seating during the evening.

In France, as the *maître d'* (headwaiter) is showing the couple to their table, the *man* precedes the lady. Also women traditionally do not pour wine (or other beverages) themselves; they should wait for either the waiter or their male companion to do so. Seating around the dining table should always alternate male, female.

More often than not, you will be well served if you ask the waiter for advice or a recommendation regarding your menu selections. Being a waiter in France is a serious occupation, and they are extremely knowledgeable about the preparation of various dishes on the menu. Unlike Los Angeles and New York, waiters are not out of work actors.

The sommelier's responsibility is to assist and advise you in perfectly matching your wine and cuisine. Do not hesitate to specify your budget.

In France it is considered good manners to keep both of your hands on the table and in sight while dining. This custom evolved in medieval times to assure that Monsieur X was not fondling Madame Y under the table.

Brits and Americans tend to be casual, loud and gregarious. This is not an issue in boisterous bars, clubs or cafés, but patrons in the higher quality dining venues tend to keep their voice level and conversation very modulated to create a subdued and pleasurable ambiance for all. When in doubt simply observe and reflect the behaviour of those around you.

Paris Rendezvous on the Web... The French lead the world in the use of online personals according to comScore Networks, an Internet research firm. Twenty two percent of French Internet users have visited a dating web site, 13 percent in the U.S. and 20 percent in Britain. Analysts suggest that online seduction appeals to the flirtatious French character.

By far the most popular online personals site in France is Meetic (www.meetic.com), with 2.3 million French visitors in a single month. By charging only men for the service (women participate for free) the site incorporates the real-world approach utilized by singles bars everywhere (focus on the women, and the men will follow).

Meetic's proprietary technology is able to search entries in 17 different languages across the entire European database of 18 million users. Meetic offers three online dating services: www.meetic.com for the general audience; www.superlov.com for young adults and www.ulteem.com for more mature users.

Web matchmakers say an emerging trend is for travelers from North America to arrange dates before they depart for Europe. They find these cross-cultural opportunities for romance an appealing alternative to meeting in bars and clubs.

Another well regarded online service is FrenchFriendFinder (http:/frenchfriendfinder.com), which was voted the "Best Online Personals Dating Service" by *Forbes* magazine. It is available in English and French.

For more traditional options, there are the personal ads in the Paris-based English language publication FUSAC (an acronym for French USA Contacts). It is distributed free at English language outlets throughout Paris. Should you prefer the services of the traditional dating and introduction service, we recommend:

UNICIS Paris

55 Boulevard des Batignolles, 8th Arr.
Tel: 01 42 94 20 20
info@unicisparis.com
www.unicis.fr

Chapter Three:
French Attitudes–Sex & Sexuality

Chapter Three:

"People who are in love suspect nothing or everything."

~ *Honoré de Balzac (1799–1850)* ~

In February 2006, l'Institut Français d'Opinion Publique (Ifop) conducted a survey about the sex lives of Parisians. Among the findings:
43% of Parisians have checked into a hotel just to have sex
7% of Parisians say they like to have their neighbors hear them having sex
35% of Parisians have had sex in a public place (parks, etc)
14% state that they have had sex in a nightclub
Almost 50% of all Parisians have been in a sex shop at least once
63% of 25–34 year olds see themselves as "adventurous" in their sex lives

The top sexual fantasy of Parisians (Selected from a list provided):
36% of Parisians said they dreamed of having sex in a limousine with tinted windows while driving up the Avenue des Champs Élysées
14% preferred the ladies fitting room of a department store
9% wanted to do it on the lawn of the Presidential Palace
13% preferred the roof of Notre Dame

Another international survey on sex, religion and infidelity asked, "Do your religious beliefs affect your sexual behavior?" For the French, "91% stated that they did not and only 3% agreed they did. Almost 40% of Americans stated that their religion affected their sexual behavior." (Euro *RSCG Worldwide)*

The French are Different than Us... "French women have always had a singular allure about them. It's not so much their total lack of body fat or those pert little breasts that can fit into the rim of a champagne glass. It's their infuriating poise and inscrutable sensuality that has captived us for centuries. 'A comparison of Amazons to Angels' is how Thomas Jefferson characterized the difference between the liberated French woman and the virtuous American maidens of the time. Since then, Americans have rushed to France in search of intellectual freedom, good food, and good sex (not necessarily in that order)." (Debra Ollivier, *France vs America: The Sex Front,* Salon.com, 2003)

Author Helena Frith Powell says of French women "One of the reasons French women spend most of their time trying to look so good is to stop their girlfriends seducing their husbands. There is much more rivalry and much less solidarity between them than between English girlfriends. In England it's a given that you're not going to try to seduce your best friend's boyfriend; here it is assumed that you are."

"American women are most often focused on their long-term happiness—marriage, family, children—and this focus obviously affects their attitude toward relationships. French women on the other hand, tend to live more 'in the moment,' believing that overall happiness in life can be very fleeting so short-term passion can be justifiable and even fulfilling." (Helena Frith Powell *Two Lipsticks and a Lover, 2006*).

French women rarely go out in groups for the female bonding experience (girl's night out) commonly seen abroad. While they certainly have girlfriends, they just seem to prefer the friendship of men to that of women. If they want female companionship, they usually opt to spend time with their female relatives. Some foreign women residing in France have found this profound difference in attitude difficult to adjust to.

French men are also quite different from their Anglophone counterparts. One significant difference is that they are much less inclined to trade in their middle-aged wives for a younger model. This marital stability permits a French wife the ultimate luxury of aging gracefully in the comfort of her home and in the bosom of her family. Thus, the permissive attitude toward sexual infidelity appears to indirectly contribute to a lower divorce rate. Which certainly raises the question: is North American style "serial marriage" and instant divorce the superior path to long-term happiness?

"Marriage is an institution necessary to the maintenance of society but contrary to the laws of nature."

~ Honore de Balzac - French novelist 1799–1850 ~

The Etiquette of Infidelity... Attitudes regarding sexual infidelity are not as strict in Europe, and in France the social framework of the matrimonial bond is often quite different than that in *bourgeois* America. The family remains a very strong and viable institution in France, and naturally French couples fall in love, marry and raise families just like anyone else, but there is more ambivalence toward the traditional constructs of marriage. The French couple exhibits a keen sense of individuality between partners with more space provided to maintain a separate identity. Accordingly, the ideal is held to be a commitment to love and security but not necessarily to absolute sexual fidelity, which is seen by many to be unrealistic over a 30, 40 or 50 year marriage. Particularly when they have children, the survival of the family unit is considered to be the highest priority.

The concept of the French couple was legally redefined by the French National Assembly in 1999 when it approved the *Pacte Civil de Solidarité*, a registered cohabitation agreement providing many of the rights and obligations, but none of the burdensome religious connotations of traditional marriage. The plain fact is that in France today a certain percentage of couples get married or use the Pacte simply to quality for the tax advantages.

A married man or woman maintaining a mistress or lover does so with the understanding that he or she will remain discreet to avoid embarrassment to their spouse. A significant percentage of French affairs are conducted between individuals who are both married, creating a sense of illicit equilibrium. An Institute of Public Opinion (IFOP) survey reveals that about 40 percent of men and 25 percent of women have extramarital affairs; however many observers believe these figures still underestimate the level of French infidelity, particularly among women.

In recent years, there has been has been a wider acceptance of the notion of mutual infidelity. The time-honored tradition was that every Frenchman had a mistress and French wives compliantly accepted this state of affairs (pun intended). However, the modern French woman now strives for equality in personal pleasure and the allure of illicit adventures. Infidelity is seen as a way to reaffirm her desirability as a woman and temporarily escape from a lukewarm marriage. While they may have been obliged to play a secondary role through much of French history, the French woman is now among the most sexually liberated in the world. They have emerged as an empowered, self-confident force to be reckoned with.

Count Vronsky in Tolstoy's *Anna Karenina* may have perfectly captured French sensibilities when he mused, "In the eyes...of all society people he ran no risk of being ridiculous. He knew very well that...the role of a man who attached himself to a married woman and devoted his life to involving her in adultery at all costs, had something beautiful and grand about it and could never be ridiculous."

This laissez-faire approach functions flawlessly because husbands, wives, mistresses and lovers each play their part in the drama generally without angst or recrimination.

"In Paris every man must have had a love affair. What woman wants something that no other woman ever wanted?"

~ Francois de la Rochefoucauld 1613–1680 ~

The Etiquette of Infidelity—France

1. Discretion is the one of the most fundamental obligations for French couples. So any overt or public affair in French society is highly discouraged. Sexual infidelity should always remain a private matter.

2. Don't ask, don't tell, no guilt. Deny, deny, deny. A spouse should never admit to having had an affair. Obviously, no self-respecting husband or wife should ever voluntarily come forward with a conscience-stricken confession begging for forgiveness. This is simply not the French style.

3. Assure your spouse of your everlasting love and devotion. It is prudent to continue to satisfy your spouse's sexual desires even though you may be having an affair.

4. Throughout France itemized home telephone bills list only the first few digits of telephone numbers called, conveniently protecting married persons who may have indiscreetly dialed their mistress or lover from home.

5. Longer term extramarital affairs are seen as preferable to one-night stands, as long as the stability of the marriage remains unthreatened. In France it is considered unseemly to fall in love with your mistress or lover given that the entire *raison d'être* (purpose) of an affair is to gratify your sexual needs, not your romantic yearnings.

6. The French believe in aging gracefully so cosmetic surgery is not a viable option for retaining your sex appeal.

7. The time established by custom for *Parisiens* and *Parisiennes* to meet their mistress or lover is between 5pm and 7pm (an interlude famously referred to as the *cinq à sept*), conveniently ensuring that one can arrive home in time for the traditional French evening meal with the entire family.

8. Forget marriage and family counseling. It is considered to be none of their damn business.

9. Infidelity is not a legal basis for divorce under French law; therefore, it is not usually raised as an issue in court.

10. Those involved in extramarital affairs are rarely caught or exposed because no one appears to be engaged in an effort to catch or expose them.

11. French fashion and lifestyle magazines encourage a married woman who is sexually unfulfilled to indulge her passions with a no-strings-attached adventure. Take a separate vacation to find a lover.

12. Forget seeking the guidance of your priest since religious doctrine influences the sexual behavior of a minuscule percentage of the French population.

The Etiquette of Infidelity—America

1. Always be unconditionally honest and forthright with your spouse, revealing every thought, word or deed regardless of how painful it may be. Only the most scrupulous devotion to veracity can possibly save your marriage.

2. Remain vigilant at all times and never, ever, under any circumstances, risk taking separate vacations as your spouse will surely be tempted.

3. Regardless of your actual age, it is critically important to retain your youthful appearance, so visit your cosmetic surgeon regularly for nips, tucks, lifts, liposuction and Botox.

4. Infidelity is morally wrong, but should you stray, sexually satisfying one-night stands are preferable to long-term affairs since they present less of a risk of falling in love.

5. Serial monogamous marriages are perfectly respectable. Middle-aged married men are almost expected to "trade in" their middle aged wives for a shiny, new, younger model.

6. If suspicious, employ the services of the best private detective money can buy to follow and photograph your spouse in *flagrante delicto* (in the act).

7. If at all possible expose your spouse's infidelity live on a day-time TV talk show.

8. Hire a ferocious, high-priced, divorce attorney to ensure that your spouse is legally, emotionally and financially crucified.

9. When exposed, demand that your spouse attend 24 months of marriage and family counseling with a professional therapist. Your marriage can only be saved when the errant spouse has revealed every last salacious and erotic detail.

10. And finally to assure that your philandering spouse is thoroughly humiliated; insist that he/she make a forthright confession of adultery to the full congregation at your Sunday religious services. Then solicit the caring guidance of your priest or pastor who may have had first-hand experience in the realm of illicit sexual affairs.

Repercussions... In America, the matter of infidelity rarely remains a private issue between the couple. There is little discretion shown by the participants and no overarching cultural norms guide or protect either the aggrieved party or the wayward spouse from the immense pressures brought to bear by those who claim to support reconciliation, but often urge retribution. The great "divorce-industrial complex" quickly gears up to provide an array of services to the unhappy couple including attorneys, accountants, psychiatrists, private detectives, and marriage counselors. These outside players may or may not have the couple's best interests at heart.

Like so many other cultural issues, American and French attitudes concerning marital affairs are as different as night and day.

Americans clearly do not grasp the finer points of conducting an affair; appear unable to properly revel in the rewards; and end up paying a very high price (in pain, anguish, and attorney's fees) for having had one.

Finally, U.S. political pundits have often questioned the "mysterious marriage" of Bill and Hillary Clinton, when in truth there is nothing mysterious about it at all. Anyone can see that it is a marriage built on the French model.

Politics without the Sex Scandal... Because of strict libel laws, the French media have avoided the sensational sex scandals that regularly convulse both the British and American political landscape, sweeping away the careers of politicians. While the French are just as titillated by sexual antics as anyone else, they don't expect it to destroy careers. There is an unyielding Gallic repugnance for this type of intemperate Anglo-Saxon Puritanism. They are pragmatic and don't hold their politicians to a higher standard than they hold themselves.

Examples of the dalliances of French leaders abound: François Félix Faure (President 1895–99) died of a stroke (*épectase*—death during orgasm) in the Elysée Palace while receiving oral sex from a very prominent socialite.

Edgar Faure (Prime Minister 1955–56) suggested that before he was elected various women had resisted him, but following his election, none were able to do so.

François Mitterrand (President 1981–95) actually maintained a second family with his long-time mistress and illegitimate child, yet this fact was never revealed in the media until after his death. Mitterrand's wife, his children, his mistress and her child all attended his funeral "together".

Several recent Presidents and Prime Ministers have acknowledged having affairs while in office. It was not unusual for these leaders to use state funds to wine and dine their mistresses or to fly them off to exotic destinations.

Still, a poll by TNS Sofres found that only 17 percent of French voters would hesitate to vote for a candidate who had extramarital affairs.

One French legislator suggested that suddenly exposing those in the Executive Branch, the National Assembly and Senate who are having *affaires d'amour* would essentially disenfranchise most of the existing government.

"The conflict between the need
to conceal and the will to reveal
has provided women with the
means to explore their own
sexuality and exercise an erotic
ascendancy over men.
The diverse selection of bras,
corsets, garters, stockings,
and panties is proof that
wearing just a little something
can be far more sexy than
wearing nothing at all."

~ Gilles Néret,
author of Dessous:
Lingerie as Erotic Weapon ~

Chapter Four:
Shopping–the Chic & Sexy Woman
4
Chapter Four:

Fine French Lingerie – The Unbridled Power to Seduce... The French woman has deservedly earned the distinction of being among the most fashionably dressed in the world. This, of course includes her entire foundation, the second skin, which she wears beneath her stylish outer attire. It has been suggested that this is where French women get their vaunted self-confidence. They feel good about themselves as women because they have that ultra sexy and extravagant lingerie clinging closely to their body.

Paris is home to countless fine lingerie retailers, prized for their superb workmanship, quality materials, and potent style. Naturally, taste in lingerie varies according to lifestyle, but that is what makes it so personal and intimate. Emotion, seduction and comfort are the terms French women most often use when speaking of their lingerie preferences. As you visit your local Parisian boutique, you will observe discerning French women ranging from grandmothers to teenagers examining the items of lingerie with the exacting scrutiny of a holy scholar studying the Dead Sea Scrolls. According to retail statistics, French women over the age of fifteen spend 20 percent or more of their annual fashion budget on lingerie.

Parisian women are not above an occasional, discreet flash of the garter and unsurprisingly garter belts and fine hosiery are some of the most popular items that French men purchase for their wives, girlfriends and mistresses. Women are also mad about bustiers that lace up because men immensely enjoy unlacing them.

Managers of many Parisian lingerie boutiques say that American and Anglo women appear to prefer the simplicity of pantyhose, complaining that the traditional garter belt and stockings are uncomfortable and impractical.

With that thought in mind, take a moment, close your eyes and visualize an intimate moment with your husband, boyfriend or lover.

In the subdued evening light, he is sitting on the bed studying you with rapt attention. In this scenario—you start to provocatively disrobe by slowly lowering your skirt to reveal an intimate, black, silk garter belt embroidered with petite, red roses and fine lace trim. The garter straps snugly support sheer, black stockings topped by a band of delicate, matching, red lace. He cannot help but notice that your lovely thighs provide a stark and sensual contrast to the captivating garter belt and hosiery. You sit down next to him, extend your shapely leg, gently releasing the metal clasp, slowly sliding the luminous, silk stocking down to your ankle. Leaning back, you seductively invite him to help you with the other garter clasp and stocking . . .

Second scenario—you start to provocatively disrobe, slowly lowering your skirt to reveal your lower body shrink-wrapped from waist to toe in seam-free, one-piece nylon spandex pantyhose (known as tights in the UK), consisting of a high-stretch, ribbed panty with cotton gusset and therapeutic support stockings. With excitement and anticipation he runs his hand up the reinforced Lycra fabric and with sustained effort, forces it into the durable, control-top, elastic waist-band. While you wait patiently, he begins to peel and roll the tightly fitted material downward over your hips, thighs and legs. With a final push the double-covered knit fabric reaches your ankles and with only a hint of static cling you manage to kick them free.

You decide. Which of these scenarios is likely to appeal to the man in your life?

In Paris you will find extraordinarily high quality, ready-to-wear *(prêt-a-porter)* intimate apparel in boutiques and better department stores throughout the city. Luxurious, "made-to-order" lingerie can be found at several high-end, specialty boutiques.

While out and about Paris, you will often see risqué lingerie ads in the Métro stations and on small billboards. Some of the most appealing are sponsored by Aubade, one of the country's premier lingerie brands founded in 1875. The captivating "Aubade Lessons in Seduction" campaign (www.aubade.com) presents black and white ads featuring sultry lingerie models and a tag line such as "Lesson in Seduction # 32." The ad campaign has been very successful and the seductive photos are now sold as both calendars and coffee table books.

That special French blend of aesthetics, tradition, magic and style is guaranteed to renew your belief in the power of femininity.

"Since the beginning of civilization, women have worn underwear. Justified as protection, or a hygienic necessity, this 'second skin' was devised to satisfy perverse erotic instincts. A 'trap laid by Venus' to entertain and stimulate the fantasies of both the woman who wears them and the man who discovers them. Corsets, bras and panties are not utilitarian items—they are elements in a mystic ritual linking man and woman. They act as an obsessive focus for fantasy, for the sex they conceal is powerless without the decorations and seductions, which separate us from it."

~ Gilles Néret ~

Princesse Tam-Tam... 23 rue de Grenelle, 7th Arr. Métro: Rue du Bac Tel: 01 45 49 28 73

Featuring bras, camisoles, slips, tops, panties and briefs in the finest fabrics, with whimisical, seductive designs. The flirty style and reasonable prices of Princesse-Tam-Tam particularly appeals to youthful customers.

Chantal Thomass... 211 rue St-Honoré, 1st Arr. Métro: Tuileries Tél: 01 42 60 40 56

Eye-catching, intimate apparel from the celebrated designer that is naughty, coquettish and expensive. *Parisiennes* adore this boudoir-style boutique for its ravishing collection of silky bras, bloomers, merrywidows, garter belts and bustiers. Thomass has a striking gift for sexy hosiery.

Fifi Chachnil... 26 rue Cambon, 1st Arr. Métro: Concorde or Madeleine Tel: 01 42 60 38 86

Fifi's is filled with cutting edge, ultra-feminine, frilly lingerie that is bold yet tasteful. The service is impeccable. A second Fifi's location is at 231 rue Saint-Honoré, 1st Arr., Métro: Concorde.

Sabbia Rosa... 71 rue des Saints-Peres, 6th Arr. Métro: Sèvres-Babylone Tel: 01 45 48 88 37

Sabbia Rosa produces luxurious lingerie for a very select clientele including Madonna, Claudia Schiffer, Isabelle Adjani, and Naomi Campbell. Chic and sensual, she uses only the finest quality materials, fabrics and lace. Ready-to-wear and made-to-order.

Alice Cadolle... 14 rue Cambon, 1st Arr. Métro: Concorde or Madeleine Tel: 01 42 60 94 94

This legendary lingerie boutique has been run by members of the same family since 1889 when the founder Herminie Cadolle invented and patented the brassiere, thus liberating French women from the corset. Her new invention was a great success during the Paris World's Fair of 1900. Cadolle produces a full range of made-to-measure intimate apparel including bustiers, teddies, panties, pajamas and sexy camisoles. The shop has catered to couture clients from across the globe including the late Princess Diana, Christina Onassis, Catherine Deneuve and Coco Chanel.

Daniela in Love... 15 rue Boissy d'Anglas, 8th Arr. Métro: Concorde Tél: 01 42 65 02 52

An innovative boutique offering a wide range of *accoutrements féminine* from petite thongs to full silk robes laced with feathers. Among their labels are the trendy "Sexy Panties" and "Naughty Nickers." This shop is popular among fashionistas.

Secret Dessous... 74 rue de Rennes, 6th Arr. Métro: St-Sulpice Tel: 01 44 39 30 10

Located in a very fashionable area, Secret Dessous offers a wide variety of ultra-sexy lingerie at surprisingly affordable prices.

Lingerie in the Department Stores *(Les Grandes Magasins)*

Les Galeries Lafayette... 40 blvd Haussmann, 9th Arr. Métro: Havre-Caumartin Tel: 01 42 82 34 56

This grand Paris department store has an eye-popping 10,000-square-foot lingerie section with over eighty different brands of bras, corsets, bustiers, garter belts and the ever popular *string* (as the thong is known in France). For a full range of prices, this store is an ideal choice. Customers are able to dim the lights in the store's stylish changing rooms, allowing you to see what your new undergarments will look like in a real world environment. In the past, Galeries Lafayette has gone so far as to offer "strip tease classes" to its female clientele, tought by competent professionals. The sold out classes were attended by 400 well-dressed, young Parisians.

Au Printemps... 64 blvd Haussmann, 9th Arr. Métro: Havre-Caumartin Tel: 01 42 82 50 00

Another of the leading department stores is distinguished by their famous stained glass cupola. Their recently renovated lingerie department is vast and very smart. Among their selection is the brand *Agent Provocateur* that includes knickers, corsets, bras, garters and those, "oh so beguiling" masks. To complement the selection of lingerie, Printemps features the largest beauty care department in the world.

Le Bon Marché... 38 rue de Sevres, 7th Arr. Métro: Sèvres-Babylone Tel: 01 44 39 80 00

This is the elegant Parisian department store that invented the very concept of chic "department shopping" in the mid–19th century. An extensive selection of intimate apparel from all of the major designers can be found in the sumptious lingerie section on the third floor. The well-appointed dressing rooms even have a telephone to conviently summon your sales assistant. The store is a favorite of well-heeled locals. While in the neighborhood, be sure to visit Le Bon Marché's enormous food hall *(La Grande Epicerie de Paris)* which offers the most extravagant selection of gourmet delicacies to be found in the capital.

Petit Bateau... 116 Avenue Champs Elysées, 8th Arr. Metro: Georges V Tel: 01 40 74 02 03

Spunky *Parisiennes* like to occasionally change the mood, so they may temporarily set aside their fancy lingerie and slip on old-fashioned, cotton briefs *(la culotte un peu grand)* for their paramour. Why dress down in this girlish attire? This adolescent look subconsciously appeals to a man's teenage fantasies. However, not just any cotton briefs will do, they must be the *Petit Bateau* brand from the very smart (and expensive), *juvénile* boutique of the same name. (Multiple locations throughout Paris).

Online Lingerie Shopping – Petite Coquette... If you wish to peruse the various brands before you go shopping visit the exquisite lingerie site *Petite Coquette* http://boutiques.petite-coquette.co.uk.

A Primer for Men – How to Purchase the Perfect Lingerie for your Wife, Girlfriend, or Mistress... French men innately understand that the purchase of a perfect lingerie ensemble for that special woman can be a romantic and well appreciated gesture. If you pay strict attention to the details and get it right there will be significant rewards. Get it wrong, such as selecting a garment that is the wrong size (as in - too *large*) or one that is "inappropriate" for her particular taste and you will live to deeply regret it. Our advice to men on how to get it right every time:

1. It is critical to know her correct bra size (chest and cup), her waist size and perhaps her color and style preferences. Simply peek in her lingerie drawer and copy down the sizes of her bra, panties, stockings and sleepwear.

2. Does she usually wear tightly fitted or loosely fitted undergarments?

3. Don't lose sight of the comfort factor. There needs to be a balance between comfort and sex appeal.

4. When shopping for lingerie, pay very close attention to the quality of the fabric and the workmanship. The softest and most luxurious fabrics are silk, satin, and cashmere (usually for women's robes). Fine lingerie with embroidered Chantilly lace is always a classic choice. Dark colors are slimming, while light colors may draw attention to potential bulges. Women prefer matching lingerie sets because an entirely coordinated ensemble is incredibly sexy and feminine. Keep in mind that just because it is the most expensive item in the store, this does not necessarily make it the best choice for your partner.

5. Perhaps the most important consideration; be sure that the items you choose will flatter her particular figure. It should make her feel attractive and appealing. Men tend to make lingerie purchases to satisfy their own personal fantasies and at times this is certainly appropriate. However, women appear to be most appreciative of an intimate gift that suits *her* needs, even though you will surely enjoy the benefits. So when in doubt, it is best to let the gift make more of a romantic than an erotic statement (unless of course, she has indicated a desire for some really, kinky lingerie).

6. Another pleasurable approach is to personally take her to your favorite lingerie boutique, ask her to model various items, and then purchase something that appeals to both of you.

The "Last Word" on Lingerie... Should you have the desire to learn a whole lot more about lingerie, a savvy French author named Gilles Néret has published two fascinating books that explore the history and evolution of undergarments and the obsessive fantasies they stimulate. These intelligent and provocative volumes delve deeply into the mythological and mystical relationship between man, woman and lingerie. The two titles are:

1000 Dessous—A History of Lingerie, Author: Gilles Néret... "Women have always known how to stimulate the latent fetishism of the men around them. Under her dress, a Greek girl of the classical period would wear a belt around her hips which was of no practical use except to draw attention to her femininity. Likewise, the women of Rome already wore garters round their thighs, though the stocking had not yet been invented. In our own century, vamps, starlets, pin-ups and models have filled our screens, our advertisements, our office calendars and our imaginations with the erotic engineering of the garter belt and the surreptitious rustle of nylon stockings."

"*1000 Dessous* traces the evolution of this living mythology from its first steps in the dawn of civilization to its apotheosis in the films and advertising campaigns of the modern world. Lavishly illustrated, it is a richly aphrodisiacal meditation, and intimate exploration of the props of our theatre of desire." Language: English

Dessous: Lingerie as Erotic Weapon, Author & Editor: Gilles Néret... The best highlights from the title *1000 Dessous* have been culled together for a delightful summary of the evolution of undergarments from the dawn of civilization to the current day. "Pleasure would perish without censorship," says French author Gilles Néret. English/French/German/Japanese—*Dessous* means undergarment in French.

To purchase the English language version of these books go to either W.H. Smith or Brentano's Bookstore, both located on rue de Rivoli (1st Arrondissement), or the Village Voice Bookstore at 6 rue Princesse (6th Arrondissement).

Zen of the High Heel... What is it about shoes? What makes a woman so sexually alluring when she is wearing just the right pair of high-heeled shoes?

Physiologically the answer is actually uncomplicated. The canting of the heel considerably higher than the toe causes the female buttocks to protrude, the bosom to lift and the waist to appear thinner. Obviously, high-heeled shoes make a woman appear taller than her true height, but just as important, they make her frame seem more curvaceous.

"Simply put shoes outwardly represent a non-verbal sign of gender, presence, and individuality. They appear unparalleled in their ability to reveal the personality of the wearer. Today footwear communicates general values, personality traits, roles and goals. Our psychological and cultural values are an expression of our spirit and are well served by our footwear. They influence the way we think, feel, and act as well as how we react to others." (Cameron Kippen)

The Debut of the High Heel Shoe... In 1533, Catherine de Medici traveled from Florence to Paris for her celebrated marriage to the *Duc d'Orléans* (Duke of Orleans).

Consistent with aristocratic marriages of the period, Catherine's betrothal was the result of an arrangement between her noble family and the French Royal family. The *Duc* (later Henry II) was destined to become the next King of France and Catherine would be his Queen.

But young Catherine was apprenhensive about her introduction to the cultivated French court. How could an ordinary teenager charm the fashionable lords and ladies of Paris? Although, thin, plain and short in stature (just under 5 feet), Catherine yearned to make a grand entrance at her first French ball. In the end, she sought the aid of a clever Florentine artisan and he promised to find a way to captivate both King and court.

The wedding was even more magnificent than she had imagined. Following the ceremony there was a hush as she entered the grand ballroom. All of those present were spellbound by the Florentine Queen. There was something highly provocative about her seductive gait. The men were entranced and the women were green with envy.

The Queen's rousing success and the introduction of the high-heeled shoe was the masterstroke of an exceptionally talented Italian cobbler who helped a modest, 14 year old girl conquer and bewitch the sophisticated French.

Sexy Shoes & Boots *(Chaussures & Bottes)*... As Catherine de Medici so aptly demonstrated, Paris is a fashion stage and women are the central players. Whatever the social setting, the costume must be appropriate to the occasion. Women have long had an abiding obsession with footwear. Naturally most men are beguiled by a well-turned leg and shapely foot, properly fitted with a sleek pair of pumps or thigh-high boots. These are our favorite footwear boutiques in Paris:

Sergio Rossi... 22 rue de Grenelle, 7th Arr. Métro: St-Sulpice Tel: 01 42 84 07 24

This small boutique in St-Germain-des-Prés is known for its outrageously sensual footwear including a selection of ultra-spiked heels. The Italian Rossi is said to be the "master of the sexiest and most erotic shoes on the planet."

Maria Luisa... 4 rue Cambon, 1st Arr. Métro: Concorde Tel: 01 47 03 48 08

Established by Venezuelan fashion maven Maria Luisa Poumallou in 1988, this elegant boutique carries all of the top designers including Manolo Blahnik.

Christian Louboutin... 38 rue de Grenelle, 7th Arr. Métro: Rue du Bac Tel: 01 42 22 33 07

Very sexy, very feminine and very hot designs by Christian Louboutin. This is a favorite fashionista boutique where Nicole Kidman and Diane von Furstenberg shop. Made-to-order *(sur le measure)* shoes and boots.

Michel Perry... 4 rue des Petits-Pères, 2nd Arr. Métro: Bourse Tel: 01 42 44 10 07

This rose-colored boutique in a boudoir-style has long been a destination for women seeking that killer "look." Known especially for his extraordinarily sensual, high leather boots, the collection also includes ankle boots, platforms, and sling-back sandals in many bright colors. "I design for women of all ages who love to be feminine and seductive, but refuse to be fashion victims," says Perry.

Ernest Chausseur... 75 blvd de Clichy, 9th Arr. Métro: Blanche Tel: 0145 26 97 20

Founded in 1804, this "specialist in high heels" *(talons haut)* features a fine selection of stilettos, platforms, mules and long boots. Heels range from 3 inches to 8 inches (8 cm to 20 cm).

Colette... 213 rue Saint-Honoré, 1st Arr. Métro: Tuileries Tel: 01 55 35 33 90 www.colette.fr

While not exclusively a shoe store, Colette is hip and edgy, selling fashion (including shoes) from both new and established designers. The very popular boutique features a wide and random collection of "accessories."

For genuine shoe bargains... An entire street lined with inexpensive shoe boutiques can be found on rue Meslay, 3rd Arr. Metro: République.

Men... And finally not to overlook the footwear needs of gentlemen—fine *prêt-a-chausser* (ready-made) and made-to-measure shoes are available at:

Berluti Shoes— 26 rue Marbeuf, 8th Arr., Métro: Franklin D. Roosevelt, Tel: 01 43 59 51 10.

Department Stores... All of the major department stores listed in the chapter on lingerie also feature extensive shoe departments.

Designer Sex Boutiques for the Ladies *(Les Sex Toys)*... One of the new trends in Paris is the emergence of chic designer sex boutiques catering exclusively to the needs and special sensibilities of contemporary women. These new up market boutiques, located on fashionable shopping streets, provide a refined and welcoming atmosphere where women can shop for sexy apparel and erotic toys *(les sex toys)* designed specifically for women.

Rykiel Woman... 4 rue de Grenelle, 7th Arr. Métro: St-Sulpice Tel: 01 49 54 66 21 http://soniarykiel.com

Nathalie Rykiel, daughter of French fashion designer Sonia Rykiel is the owner of this chic, adults-only lingerie and sex boutique. Every accessory that a sexy and savvy female might require can be found in this well-appointed boudoir. The shop carries a wide selection of stimulating and erotic sex toys, including one indispensible gadget, the vibrating bath sponge.

And what essential fashion accessory does every glamorous woman require for her new color-coordinated vibrator? *Mais oui,* a small sequined black satin Sonia Rykiel bag to carry it in. Rykiel Women is located in the heart of the St-Germain-des-Prés shopping district.

Yoba La Boutique... 11 rue du Marché St Honoré, 1st Arr. Métro: Tuileries or Pyramides Tel: 01 40 41 04 06 www.yobaparis.com

This refined boutique located in the well-heeled rue Marché St Honoré (not far from the Place Vendôme) sells sexy lingerie, tasteful sex toys (*vibromasseurs* and *godemichets*), beauty products and jewelry. The popular shop is dedicated to female joys and pleasures say owners, Caroline Weinberg and Sophie Haftor-Helmerson. Check out the *"Canard Coquin Rose"* (pink duck), an exact copy your childhood bath toy but this one produces "powerful waves of vibration to sooth away the stresses and tensions of daily life." Ladies are invited to attend a sort of *"vibrator vernissage"* (exhibition) with their girlfriends on Thursdays between 6:00 and 9:00pm. There is also a Yoba Corner located in the famous Printemps department store on blvd Haussmann.

“Having tasted
all the pleasures of
our separate lives, let us
enjoy the happiness of
discovering that none
of them is comparable
to that which we once
experienced together,
and shall again—to find
it more delicious
than before.

~ Pierre Choderlos
de Laclos - Les Liaisons
Dangereuse ~

Chapter Five:
Hotels–Sensual & Romantic

Chapter Five:

Recommended Hotels for Lovers... Buried in a down comforter and the crisp sheets of an 18th-century four poster bed, you awaken in a cozy hotel room as the late-morning sunshine streams through the lace curtains at the tall French windows. Surrounded by antique furnishings lovingly assembled by the hotel proprietor, you gaze out at the leafy plane trees in the small walled garden. As you sip your café au lait and spread rich Normandy butter on a warm croissant, you watch the barges float down the Seine. This is the how one dreams of beginning the day in Paris.

Seeking a picture perfect hotel that oozes great charm and character for a romantic excursion with your spouse or a secret tryst with your lover? There are a number of such hotels to be found in Paris and they are available in every price category. Some are tucked away in a magical corner of an ancient cobblestone street and others are found in the center of the chic fashion district. Many offer intimate Gallic charm while others engulf you in superlative, world-class luxury. What the carefully selected hotels listed here have in common is an almost indefinable Parisian style, good taste and alluring ambiance. With a couple of exceptions, we have recommended small, boutique hotels with fewer than 30 rooms, since lodging in this category tends to appeal to the ardent and whimsical imagination of the romantic.

Depending upon the season and availability, a reduced rate for many of the hotels listed below may be found by diligently searching various travel sites on the internet. With the exception of the top tier hotels, guest rooms in Paris are generally smaller than those found in North America. The buildings are older and space is always at a premium. Still, most visitors enjoy the cozy accommodations, but if space is an issue for you, consider upgrading to a junior suite, suite or more highly rated hotel.

L'Hôtel ★★★★Luxe... Quarter: St-Germain-des-Prés, 13 rue des Beaux-Arts, 6th Arr. Métro: Odéon, Tel: 01 44 41 99 00 Fax: 01 43 25 64 81 www.l-hotel.com Rates: Double rooms from €300 Memorable rooms: 54 and 62

This may very well be the most captivating and romantic boutique hotel on the Left Bank. The period building features a 19th century circular lobby atrium rising six stories to a domed skylight. Each of the hotel's 20 opulent guest rooms have their own eclectic style and character with impeccable décor ranging from Napoleon III to Italian Baroque to Art Deco. On the top floor a sumptuously appointed penthouse apartment, with terrace, overlooks the nearby rooftops and the bellower of the church of Saint-Germain-des-Prés. The hotel is a haven of calm and splendid comfort in the center of the bustling Left Bank, steps away from antique dealers, art galleries and venues such as the famed Café de Flore.

L'Hotel is steeped in myth due to the fact that Queen Margot maintained a love-nest on this site four centuries ago. And in November 1900, shortly before expiring in suite number 16, Oscar Wilde exclaimed "My wallpaper and I are fighting a duel to the death. One or the other of us must go." Celebrities past and present including Marcello Mastroianni, Ava Gardner, Roman Polanski, Robert De Niro, and Claudia Cardinale have vied to stay in the room named after him.

Original Cocteau paintings and handwritten letters from Wilde adorn the walls of the reception. The public areas include an elegant Empire-style restaurant, bar, library, *fumoir* and a verdant courtyard. A tiled Roman-style pool, Jacuzzi and steam room can be found in the ancient vaulted cellar. In a unique romantic flourish, the management admits only two persons at a time into the pool and upon request will light the entire room with candles. Neatly tucked away on a quiet street, L'Hotel is a very rare and enchanting experience. Rooms, junior suites, suites and penthouse suite.

Victoria Palace Hotel ★★★★... Quarter: Montparnasse, 6 rue Blaise Desgoffe, 6th Arr. Métro: Saint Placide, Tel: 01 34 49 70 00 Fax: 01 34 49 23 75 www.victoriapalace.com Rate: doubles from €220 Memorable room: 110

Built in 1913, the Victoria Palace Hotel is located on a quiet street in the heart of the Left Bank. Behind its elegant limestone facade, the hotel is an ideal romantic retreat in the lively district of Montparnasse. The property features spacious guestrooms, doubles, junior suites, and suites, all with marble bathrooms. The tasteful decor reflects a traditional French style with fabric-covered walls and canopied beds. The warm tones of the lobby and bar-lounge are radiant with gilded stucco, crystal chandeliers and a cozy fireplace. Guests are only a few blocks from the Luxembourg Gardens, the restaurants and shops on trendy rue

Cherche Midi or Bon Marche, the most luxurious department store in the city. Complementary breakfast and concierge service.

Le Relais Saint Germain ★★★★... Quarter: St-Germain-des-Prés, 9 carrefour de l'Odéon 6th Arr. Métro: Odéon, Tel: 01 43 2912 05 Fax: 01 46 33 45 30 www.hotel-paris-relais-saint-germain.com Rates: doubles from €180

The sophisticated, country style of this boutique hotel will captivate you with its pleasing warmth and comfort. Recently purchased and renovated by Parisian chef Yves Cambeborde, the property is now attached to the highly rated bistro Le Comptoir, specialzing in the cuisine of South-west France. The hotel is well situated in the center of the bustling Saint Germain district, minutes from the Seine, Notre Dame, major museums and the smart cafes on blvd St-Germain-des-Prés. Abundant art, antiques, rich fabrics, and beamed ceilings are found throughout the hotel, creating a delightful ambiance. There are 30 guest rooms and 2 suites with marble bath available. Larger rooms have good-sized sitting areas and some feature a terrace. The Odéon metro stop is 20 meters away. Free WiFi and internet access. An accomodating and pleasant staff. Complementary breakfast.

Hotel Britannique ★★★... Quarter: Châtelet-Les-Halles, 20 avenue Victoria, 1st Arr. Metro: Châtelet-Les-Halles, Tel: 01 42 33 74 59 Fax: 01 42 33 82 65 www.hotel-britannique. fr Rates: doubles from €160

Ideally situated on a serene street a block from the Seine, the Hotel Britannique features 38 charming, soundproofed rooms and 1 junior suite. While the standard guest rooms are relatively small in size, they are handsomely decorated in rich burgundy and gold with floral tapestry curtains. In operation since 1861, this Right bank property in the very heart of historical Paris, is clean, quiet and comfortable. As the name suggests the décor is in the English country style and they provide a full English breakfast, complete with Darjeeling tea. Guests may relax in the over-stuffed leather chairs of the reading room just off the colorful lobby. Internet WiFi access is available. Perhaps the hotel's most appealing feature is its accessibility to so many of the city's prime attractions. It is a few blocks from the Louvre and five minutes from the old bridge, Pont au Change that leads to Ile de la Cité, Notre Dame and the Latin Quarter. The Châtelet-Les-Halles Metro stop is only 50 meters away. Located close to the Rue de Rivoli shopping street, there are boutiques, restaurants, cafes & bistros nearby. While there are more luxurious hotels in central Paris, with larger rooms, few quaint properties in this price range are to be found. This is an ideal choice for a couple with a moderate budget. The staff is cordial and very helpful.

Hôtel Le Bristol ★★★★ Luxe... Quarter: Faubourg Saint-Honoré, 112 rue du Faubourg St-Honore, 8th Arr. Métro: Miromesnil, Tel: 01 53 43 43 00 Fax: 01 53 43 43 01 www.lebristolparis.com Rates: Double rooms from €590

Hotel Le Bristol is ranked among the city's most luxurious "palace" hotels. The classic Art Deco façade overlooks the fashionable rue du Faubourg Saint Honoré, steps from Elysée Palace, home of the French President. The street features fine galleries, haute couture boutiques and some of the best antique shops in the city. Originally, a majestic 18th century home, the hotel is lavishly furnished with old master paintings, Gobelin tapestries and museum quality art objets. Le Bristol is known for its extraordinarily large guest rooms adorned with authentic Louis XV and XVI furniture plus Carrera marble bathrooms (complete with Hermes robes). The rooms and suites overlooking the hotel's exquisite interior garden (the largest hotel garden in Paris) are always the most popular. Some rooms offer a terrace where one may enjoy a sunny breakfast. A highly trained staff, many in service for over 20 years, provide the exceptional, world class service expected of a top luxury hotel. A member of the "Leading Hotels of the World," Le Bristol is a favorite of film stars, politicians, statesmen and business executives.

The restaurant (two Michelin stars) is the realm of celebrated chef Eric Fréchon. An enclosed swimming pool and solarium on the roof offer splendid views of Sacré Coeur and the Eiffel Tower. Additional amenities include the Anne Semonin Spa (famous for their jet-lag facials), fitness center and sauna. And at €10 for a half day, the hotel will provide guests with a Smart car for Paris shopping jaunts. Loyal hotel guests say, sure, Le Bristol is expensive but certainly worth every penny.

Hôtel des Grandes Ecoles ★★★... Quarter: Latin Quarter, 75 rue du Cardinal-Lemoine, 5th Arr. Métro: Cardinal-Lemoine, Phone: 01 43 26 79 23 Fax: 01 43 25 28 15 www.hotel-grandes-ecoles.com Rates: Double rooms from €110

Well situated on a leafy secluded property, the small family-run Hôtel des Grandes Ecoles, in the historical heart of the Latin Quarter, has the quaint, pastoral look of a Provincial inn. The accommodations, ranging in size from cozy to comfortable are decorated in vintage, country style with floral-patterned wallpaper and embroidered bedspreads. Take your breakfast under the Judas trees in the secluded, cobbledstone courtyard. The surrounding neighborhood is filled with pleasant shops, cafés and restaurants. Within walking distance is the Sorbonne, the ancient rue Mouffetard market street and the picturesque place de la Contrescarpe. The hotel has a deep literary provenance in that Ernest Hemingway lived a few doors to the South and James Joyce resided next door as he penned *Ulysses.* Hôtel des Grandes Ecoles is extraordinarily popular due to its charm and reasonable rates, so bookings should be made a minimum of 3 months in advance. No TV's or air conditioning. The most desirable rooms are numbers 29 to 33 offering direct access to the courtyard.

Pavilion de la Reine ★★★★... Quarter: Le Marais, 28 Place des Vosges, 3rd Arr. Métro: St-Paul or Bastille, Tel: 01 40 29 19 19 Fax: 01 40 29 19 20 Rates: Double rooms from €345

Blessed with an extraordinary location on the Place des Vosges, this boutique hotel is housed in a beautifully restored 17th century mansion. The building's ivy covered façade overlooks a leafy, flower filled courtyard. You will find oak beams, tapestries and fine provincial décor in the public salons. A cozy, wall-paneled sitting room is dominated by a large, stone fireplace that is in constant use in the winter months.The fifty five guest rooms, junior suites and duplex suites are individually decorated with rich fabrics, period furniture and antique four-poster beds. The modern bathrooms are spacious with wooden floors and marble baths. Breakfast is served in the ancient vaulted cellar. Shopping and fine dining are steps away under the stately arcades of the square. The Picasso Museum, the Carnavalet Museum and the attractions of the Bastille district are close at hand. Pavilion de la Reine is a member of Small Luxury Hotels of the World.

Hotel Louis II ★★★... Quarter: Odéon, 2 rue St-Sulpice, 6th Arr. Métro: Odéon, Tel: 01 46 33 13 80 Fax: 01 46 33 17 29 www.paris-hotel-louisdeux.com/index.html Rates: Double rooms from €140

A charming boutique hotel located near St-Germain-des-Prés, steps from the beautiful Luxembourg Gardens and the Carrefour de l'Odéon. This former manor house has maintained much of its 18th century character, offering cozy guest rooms with exposed wooden beams, antique furnishings and modern bathrooms. The warm tones, gilt framed mirrors and fresh flowers in the public areas glow with a provincial ambiance. Offering 22 rooms and junior suites, the hotel is an exceptional value for this upscale quarter. The attic rooms are particularly snug and romantic. Free WiFi access. After shopping at the exclusive shops in the nearby area, visit the quaint Café de la Mairie overlooking the place St-Sulpice (and the church of St-Sulpice).

Relais-Hôtel du Vieux ★★★★... Quarter: Latin Quarter, 9 rue Gît-le-Cœur, 6th Arr. Métro: St Michel, Tel: 01 44 32 15 90 Fax: 01 43 26 00 15, www.vieuxparis.com Rates: Double rooms from €235

Built in 1480 this intimate family owned hotel was the former home of the Duc d'O. Situated on a quiet side street in the Latin Quarter, it is steps away from the Seine and Notre Dame, as well as restaurants, shops, and cafes. The 12 diminutive, but romantic rooms, and 7 suites are adorned with warm, country colors, original half-timbered beams, and lots of character. Suites feature a mezzanine, marble baths with Jaccuzzi and a view of the Paris rooftops. In the 1950's and 60's, the hotel was home to writers and poets from the "Beat Generation" including Jack Kerouac, Allen Ginsberg and William S. Burroughs. Concierge service and free WiFi.

Saint James Paris ★★★★ Luxe... Quarter: Arc de Triomphe, 43 avenue Bugeaud, 16th Arr. Métro: Porte Dauphine, Tel: 01 44 05 81 81 Fax: 01 44 05 81 82 www.saint-james-paris.com Rates: Double rooms from €370

Regally situated in a walled, private park in the genteel 16th Arrondissement, this lovely Second Empire property is the only chateau hotel in Paris. The guest rooms and suites are spacious and exceptionally quiet, many providing a view of the magnificent gardens. For those in search of ultimate luxury, there are two grand duplex apartments situated in the former estate's gatehouses. The hotel is an oasis of calm in the refined embassy quarter between the Arc de Triomphe and the Bois de Boulogne. Be sure to visit the sumptuous Library Bar and restaurant, complete with 12,000 leather-bound volumes. Amenities include: concierge service, health club, solarium, hammam, and free parking.

Chapter Six:
Restaurants–Passionate Epicurean Pleasures

Chapter Six:

"Lunch kills half of Paris, supper the other half."

~ Charles de Montesquieu (1689–1755) ~

Restaurants for Lovers... In France there is the enduring sense that patrons savor their time at the table and one is never rushed by the restaurant staff. In fact, many of the finer restaurants and bistros offer only a single seating each evening, so you can enjoy the slower pace of life. There is an incomparable selection of restaurants, with new venues constantly emerging, while many traditional haunts remain popular decade after decade (some literally for centuries).

Here, the author presents a selection of his favorite, romantic Parisian restaurants. The historic architecture, the elegant décor set the proper seductive mood and the obliging staff establish the temperament of the dining ritual. In this culinary theater, it is the passionate chef who must perform nightly with gastronomic finesse and inspiration. Luxuriate in the sensual pleasure of exquisitely prepared cuisine and carefully selected wines, while dining *a deux* in the timeless city of romance.

Many restaurants open for dinner at about 7:00 or 7:30pm, but few Parisians dine before 8 or 8:30 at the earliest. Restaurants that are open for lunch will start serving around 11:30am and remain open until about 2:00 or 2:30pm. Please note that it is not uncommon for the top-rated Michelin star restaurants to be closed on weekends, the exception being those located in hotels. If you are going to Paris for a special romantic holiday and plan to dine at a popular restaurant, it is advisable to make your reservations before you depart to assure seating availability.

In the not so distant past, the proper Parisian attire for almost any dining experience was a suit and tie for the man and a dress for the lady. However, this standard is now considerably more relaxed, except in the more upscale establishments where appropriate attire is still required.

The restaurant's menu is known as the carte. The *prix fixe menu,* usually referred to as just the "menu" is a complete multi-course meal offered at a fixed price and is almost always the best value in a restaurant or bistro. Your entrée is the appetizer; the plat is the main course and dessert the final course. A cheese course is optional. Of course, dishes may be ordered individually - *à la carte*. Many bistros change the menu daily according to what is fresh, available and in season. We have selected a dozen dining establishments that provide a beguiling and seductive Parisian experience.

Recommended Restaurants:

Restaurant Lapérouse... 51 quai des Grands-Augustins, 6th Arr. Métro: St-Michel, Tel: 01 43 26 68 04, www.restaurantla-perouse.com/index.php, Hours: daily, closed Sun and for lunch Sat, Average à la carte: €30—Prix fixe menu: €105

An evening spent at the historic Left-Bank, Belle Époque restaurant Lapérouse is like being transported back to the sensual and indulgent Paris of the 18th century. This grand 235 year old former townhouse faces the River Seine and is an ideal location for a captivating and romantic dinner.

It is rare indeed to find a luxurious dining venue where you may satisfy both your gastronomic and amorous appetites simultaneously. Lapérouse has been famous (if not infamous) for centuries because on its lavish second floor are located nine very intimate private dining salons *(salons particuliers).* These secluded salons offer the ultimate in romantic dining and have long been the haunt of sophisticated Parisians seeking a discreet and passionate rendezvous. On the restaurant's elegant gilded rococo mirrors one can still see entwined hearts and dates where ladies cut into the glass to check the authenticity of their gift of diamonds.

Graced with gaslights, hand-painted ceilings and rich wall paneling, the décor is seductive in the extreme. One of the more sumptuous private salons is named after La Belle Otero, the famous Parisian courtesan and another is named after novelist Victor Hugo, a frequent guest. These salons are furnished with an intimate dining table luxuriously set for two, comfortable leather chairs and an extra plush velvet divan ideal for "relaxation." The professional waiters who serve the private salons show exceptional discretion, and may be depended upon to postpone delivery of the next course if necessary. One may also choose to be seated in the lush Belle Époque elegance of the main dining room.

At one time the kitchen was under the direction of famed chef Auguste Escoffier (1846–1935), who found himself at the very pinnacle of French gastronomy. In 1907 Lapérouse had the distinction of being the first restaurant ever to be awarded three Michelin stars. The restaurant now is in the capable hands of Chef Samuel Benne, who provides traditional haute cuisine. Style: Classic French—Specialties: The Chef excels at seafood dishes such as homard (lobster) and delicious Dublin Bay prawns. Game dishes are available in the fall. Signature dessert: Soufflé Lapérouse with wild raspberry brandy. Reservations: For this restaurant it is suggested that you make reservations very far in advance to assure seating, especially if you wish to dine in one of the private salons. (The surcharge varies according to the salon selected but is in the neighborhood of € 150. This will accord you about three hours of luxurious and romantic privacy).

Chalet des Iles... Bois de Boulogne, Lac Inférieur, 16th Arr. Métro: Rue de la Pompe, Tel: 01 42 88 04 69, www.lechaletdesiles.net, Reservation is required, Average à la carte: € 35—Prix fixe menus: €25–31

Frankly it just does not get much more idyllic than this–lunch or dinner on the terrace of a rustic restaurant, hidden away on the small island of a lake, in the middle of a 2,500-acre park (in the center of Paris). In any season this is one of the most charming and best loved dining venues in the city. On a summer day, one is surrounded by tall chestnut trees, verdant greenery and the tranquil beauty of the lake. In winter, you are ensconced in the bucolic warmth of the restaurant with a roaring fire in the fireplace, and a pianist playing softly in the background. In autumn, the turning leaves accent your dining experience.

This former hunting lodge built by Emperor Napoleon III features pastoral country décor with wicker furnishings and traditional French cuisine. In good weather a stroll along the island paths give the feeling of a glorious day in the country. Just a ten minute taxi ride from the Arc de Triomphe, access to the island is by a covered boat (free passage) that departs from the landing *(embarcaderie)* on the east side of the Lac Inférieur. If you prefer a table with a view on one of the terraces, be sure to specify this when making your reservations. Style: Traditional French fare with a number of excellent prix fixe menus.

La Maison de l'Amérique Latine... 217 blvd St-Germain, 7th Arr. Métro: Solférino, Tel: 01 49 54 75 00 Reservations: 01 49 54 75 10, Prix fixe menus: €32–37, Lunch and dinner

Restaurant is open only between the 1st of May and the 30th of September.

This splendid restaurant is located within the ancient grounds of the Latin American Museum *(La Maison de l'Amérique Latine).* The enchanting 18th century walled garden is full of towering lime trees providing guests with a quiet refuge from the hustle and bustle of St-Germain-des-Prés. A candlelight dinner on the terrace overlooking the garden should be followed by a romantic stroll around the grounds. The prix fixe menu of traditional French cuisine changes frequently and is reasonably priced.

Restaurant Le Bristol (Michelin—2 Stars)... In the Hotel Le Bristol, 112 rue du Faubourg-St-Honoré, 8th Arr. Métro: Miromesnil, Tel: 01 53 43 43 00 www.lebristolparis.com, Dress code: Jacket & tie, Average à la carte: €65—Prix fixe menus: €75 & 160, Hours: Mon–Sun: noon to 2:00pm & 7:00 to 10:30pm

This breathtaking French temple of gastronomy is located in the fashionable Faubourg-St-Honoré (embassy row district). You feel as if you have been transported back a few centuries to dine in a fine Parisian palace. The talented chef Eric Fréchon is a past winner of the Meilleur Ouvrier de France award for culinary art and was voted "Best Chef in Paris in 2003." The restaurant lies within the confines of the luxurious Hotel Le Bristol (a 5-star property). A distinguishing characteristic of Le Bristol is that the location of their restaurant shifts with the change of seasons. The Winter Restaurant is open from November to April while the Summer Restaurant is open from May to October.

These two peerless dining venues are perfectly reflective of their respective seasons. The Winter Restaurant *(Restaurant d'Hiver)* is situated in an elegant oval room ornamented with carved, Hungarian oak paneling accented with antique panels painted by Gustave-Louis Jaulmes. A combination of subtle lighting, deep carpets and the innate warmth of the wood exude a glowing sense of harmony with bright touches of color provided by stunning floral arrangements. The sense of gentility is accentuated by a table set with elegant Haviland-Limoges porcelain and Christofle silver flatware.

The Summer Restaurant *(Restaurant d'Été)* is housed within a handsome glass pavilion with massive floor-to-ceiling windows facing the hotel's sumptuous 13,000-square-foot garden (the largest hotel garden in Paris). Featuring blond wood seating and crisp white linen, the refined décor is an inviting summer retreat, where light and soft shadows play. With the first rays of sunshine, tables shaded by large white, Italian-style parasols are set up on the garden terrace for refined al fresco dining.

Chef Fréchon directs a kitchen staff of 120 utterly dedicated to the French culinary craft and providing absolutely impeccable "Old World" service. As we know, ambiance, memorable cuisine and fine wine combine to create an aura of romance. Fréchon works culinary wonders with crayfish, scallops, eel, Normandy beef, lamb and his specialty *homard Breton* (blue lobster from Brittany)—served with curried cucumber and coconut milk. Another signature dish is *challandais* duck breast roasted with spices, pineapple ravioli, lime and grated mango, accompanied with souffléed potatoes. Memorable deserts include a zabaglione (custard) of dark chocolate with caramel, bourbon-infused ice cream and a touch of Caribbean spices. Finish with a selection of exquisite cheeses provided by the famed Fromagerie Cantin. The restaurant offers an extensive selection of fine wines and Champagne from a cellar containing 31,000 bottles.

Restaurant Le Bristol has been the author's favorite Paris restaurant for a number of years.

La Fontaine de Mars... 129 rue Saint-Dominique, 7th Arr. Métro: École Militaire, Tel: 01 47 05 46 44, Hours: Open for lunch and dinner 7 days a week. Reservations required, Average à la carte: €35–42

A superb traditional Parisian bistro in the tony 7th Arrondissement. Serving delicious Gascon-style cuisine from the French Southwest, La Fontaine de Mars has very cozy surroundings with lace curtains and checked table cloths. The upstairs tables are slightly more elegant and tables are available outside in good weather. Christine, the charming owner, provides a very friendly welcome and service is perfect. Specialties: Try the delicious duck breast *(magret de canard)*, the cassoulet or the fricassée of chicken with wild morel mushrooms in a cream sauce. Finish with a *tarte tatin* (apple tart) with homemade vanilla ice cream. Wines include selections from Chinon in the Loire and Madiran in the Basque region. Before or after dinner, stroll down the famous market street on nearby rue Cler. This is one of the author's favorite small bistros.

Le Coupe-Chou... 9 rue de Lanneau, 5th Arr. Métro: Maubert-Mutualité Tel: 01 46 33 68 69 Open daily: a la carte prices: €25–50—Prix fixe menus: €24 & 32

You enter the medieval, stone walled room through an almost hidden doorway off a narrow, cobbled passageway. A massive fireplace warms the space with a crackling log fire. Beamed ceilings, stone floors and period furnishings abound as you wind your way through a succession of enchanting rooms, each with its own unforgettable décor. The restaurant, mostly lit by candlelight and the many fireplaces, oozes atmosphere. The ancient ivy-covered building dating from the 15th century is located in the Latin Quarter, not far from the Sorbonne. Le Coupe-Chou offers a classic home-style French menu, efficient service and a warm welcome. Specialties: *Bœuf Bourguignon,* Steak Tartare, duck confit, salmon, and rack of lamb. After dinner repair to the cozy stone-vaulted bar for a Cognac or Armagnac. In French "Coupe-Chou" means cut cabbage.

Le Grand Vefour (Michelin—2 Stars)... Inside the Palais Royal, 17 rue de Beaujolais, 1st Arr. Métro: Palais Royal–Musée du Louvre, Tel: 01 42 96 56 27, Dress code: Jacket & tie, Hours: closed Fri evening, Sat and Sun, Average à la carte: €30—Prix fixe menu: €80 to 250

Le Grand Vefour is set among the historic colonnaded arcades of the 18th century Palais Royal (near the Louvre) and overlooks the palace's interior garden. This is another French gastronomic temple for international foodies. The sumptuous restaurant encompasses more than 200 years of French history, having welcomed Napoleon and Josephine Bonaparte, Voltaire, Victor Hugo, Alexander Dumas, Henri Balzac, Frederic Chopin, Jean-Paul Sartre, Simone de Beauvoir, and a host of other legendary writers, artists and statesmen. Among its patrons were the French intellectuals who plotted the revolution of 1789. Its kitchen and the professional staff of servers and sommeliers are overseen by Master Chef Guy Martin who prepares traditional French cuisine favoring his native Savoie region. Specialties: foie gras raviolis with truffle cream and wild duck cooked in laurel leaves with fig juice. Desserts include the restaurant's signature artichoke crème brûlée. The restaurant has an exceptional wine cellar.

Over the past two centuries Le Grand Vefour has had many illustrious owners, but is now a property of the famed Taittinger family, producers of Taittinger Champagne.

Le Pré Catelan (Michelin—3 Stars)... Routes de Suresnes, Bois de Boulogne, 16th Arr. Tel: 01 44 14 41 14 Métro: Porte Dauphine, Hours: Tues–Sun noon–2.30pm, Tues–Sat 8:00 to 10.30pm, Reservations required, Dress code: Jacket & tie required, à la carte: €120 to 140—Prix fixe menus: €80 & 180

An elegant and stylish restaurant located in the lush woodland setting of the Bois de Boulogne. The feeling is that you are dining deep in the French countryside. The kitchen is in the hands of inventive French Chef Frédéric Anton, once an assistant to the great Joel Robuchon. For romantic ambiance on clear, balmy nights, one can dine on the garden terrace, under the star-studded sky. In winter, dine around the cozy crackling fireplace. Specialties: Languostine ravioli in a foie gras crème with black truffles; dessert specialties include apples braised with caviar, fine blinis, and cream beaten with fresh herbs.

Auberge Etchegorry... 41 rue Croulebarbe, 13th Arr. Métro: Corvisart, Tel: 01 44 08 83 51, Open daily except Sun & Mon, Average à la carte price: €32 –35—Prix fixe menu: €20 to 25

This atmospheric *auberge* (inn) located near the Gobelin tapestry workshops serves traditional Southwestern cuisine (Basque). The restaurant is situated in an ancient two-story house graced with smoked hams and twined garlic hanging from the rafters. The hearty menu includes specialties such as authentic paella, *cassoulet, magret* of duckling, *piperade* (a typical Basque omelet of tomatoes and peppers), cocottes of mussels and delicious pan-fried slices of foie gras. Wines from the Pyrénées region perfectly complement your meal. This restaurant is often filled with those in search of fabulous country cuisine at a very moderate price, so make reservations in advance.

Les Élysées du Vernet (Michelin—2 Stars)... In the Hôtel Vernet, 25 rue Vernet, 8th Arr. Métro: George V, Tel: 01 44 31 98 98, Prix fixe menus: €60 to130

An awe-inspiring classic French gem located in the Hotel Vernet. Reserve a candle-lit table in the intimate, arcaded dining room, beneath the magnificent *verrière* (glass-domed ceiling) designed by none other than Gustave Eiffel. Chef Eric Briffard, a student of Robuchon, focuses on French haute cuisine. Specialties: *Epaul d'agneau aux aromates* (herb-flavored lamb from the Lozère region), *homard bleu cuit sur la braise* (rosemary-infused blue lobster on the grill), *salade de St Jacques au Yuzu* (scallop salad with Yuzu). An exhaustive wine list and delightful desserts round out the menu. Lunch is more affordable (€48 or €65 for the prix fixe menu). Reservations are essential—and to enjoy the full experience of this restaurant's fine architecture, reserve at least a week in advance specifying the "main dining room."

Le Train Bleu Restaurant... In the Gare de Lyon (train station), place Louis Armand, 12th Arr. Métro: Gare de Lyon, Tel: 01 43 43 09 06, www.le-train-bleu.com, Average à la carte price: €66—prix fixe menus: €45 & 85 including a half bottle of wine

This sumptuous restaurant decorated in a breathtaking Second-Empire style was built on the second floor of the Gare de Lyon train station during the Belle-Époque. It was part of the vast construction for the 1900 Universal Exhibition along with the Grand Palais, the Petit Palais and other landmarks. The décor is a masterpiece of gilt, sculpture, dark wood paneling, and crystal chandeliers. Featuring forty-one massive Impressionist ceiling frescoes, Le Train Bleu was classified as a national historic treasure in 1972. It has served as a location for countless films including Luc Besson's *Nikita.* It is an ideal venue for a romantic rendezvous or an afternoon apertif. Traditional French cuisine. Specialties: Lamb and veal dishes.

And finally for those who may enjoy a rather naughty dining experience, there is:

Autrement... chez soi... 97 rue de Cléry, 2nd Arr. Métro: Bonne-Nouvelle, Tel: 06 50 87 20 00, www.autrement-chez-soi.com, Hours: Lunch – noon to 4:00pm Mon to Fri, Dinner – Mon to Sat starting at 9:00pm, Closed Sun, Average à la carte: €22—Prix fixe menu: €50 & 60

This well-turned out, but decidedly eccentric venue declares itself to be a "restaurant coquin & lounge club," which is to say, a gathering place of the naughty and mischievous. The establishment is located in a five story, architecturally distinctive corner building in the shape of a narrow triangle, like a miniature of the "Flat Iron Building" in New York. The imaginative Autrement... chez soi is designed to satisfy one's gastronomic and carnal appetites all in a single setting. The décor could be described as classic French but with a roguish designer twist. The restaurant serves gourmet cuisine prepared by a veteran Parisian chef. The menu changes with the season but customarily includes a variety of fish and beef dishes (including lobster) along with a very solid wine and champagne list.

At the ground floor entry, the small bar is ideal for a pre-dinner drink. Dinner is served in the stylish restaurant on the next floor. Above the restaurant is an intimate dance floor, bar and lounge featuring some of the most comfortable and unusual armchairs you are ever likely to encounter in France. The next level is an inviting playroom and on the top floor, a cozy nook neatly nestled under the mansard roof.

After a satisfying meal, patrons repair to the upper floors to amuse themselves, their intimate companions and the other guests strolling through. Reservations are obligatory (best made 48 hours in advance) – Maximum capacity 12 couples. Autrement chez soi translates as "otherwise at home" which pretty neatly sums up the whimsical atmosphere.

Cafés – Life in the Slow Lane... We recommend only a few of our favorite cafés. As with art, and sex everyone develops his or her own personal preferences. Note: while in the past, it often seemed that smoking was mandatory for any café habitué, it has been banned as of January 2008.

Café de Flore... 172 blvd St-Germain, 6th Arr. Métro: St-Germain-des-Prés, Tel: 01 45 48 55 26, Expensive.

The Flore remains a classic among sophisticated locals and visitors from around the world. In many ways, it is a perfect mirror of Parisian society. The famous terrace facing blvd St-Germain des Pres is the ideal spot to chill out; to see and be seen. Few patrons are unaware of the deep history of the Flore and that it was the favored hangout of Sartre and Beauvoir. The cafe has changed little since opening in 1913. The menu offers splendid salads and delicious café fare. Consume a dozen oysters and a bottle of Champage on a sunny Sunday afternoon while watching the world stroll by; it simply doesn't get any better. The cozy rooms above the café host a philosophy discussion in English on the first Wednesday of the month – 8:00pm.

Café Charbon... 109 rue Oberkampf, 11th Arr. Métro: Parmentier, Tel: 01 43 57 55 13, Moderate.

The beautifully restored Belle-Époque café is located in the trendy Oberkampf district. Renovation of this single building served to launch a renaissance of the entire quarter. Café Charbon features high ceilings, a cavernous dining room, large mirrors and subdued lighting. Wildly popular with the young, laid-back, bohemian crowd, the café features modest drink and food prices served by an attentive staff. The Sunday brunch is well attended.

La Palette... 42 rue de Seine, 6th Arr. Métro: Mabillon, Tel: 01 43 26 68 15, Moderate.

This is the very model of the French-style café, featuring a wonderfully worn ambiance with eccentric but friendly waiters. It is frequented by a devoted crowd of locals and visitors alike. A good spot to down a few glasses of pastis and the plat de jour. Patrons seated on the terrace overlook the narrow confines of rue de Seine, while the atmosphere at the zinc bar inside is crowded and boisterous. The ancient room behind the bar reeks with character and is a bit more subdued.

Le Café du Marché... 38 rue Cler, 7th Arr. Métro: École Militaire, Tel: 01 47 05 51 27, Inexpensive.

Café du Marché is perfect for an inexpensive lunch or dinner while exploring the lively rue Cler market street. Tables and chairs spill out onto the picturesque cobblestone street in good weather and retreat under the closed canopy in winter. County-style daily specials are posted on the chalkboard. Choose from a superb selection of salads (try the one with foie gras and Parma ham) or the plat de jour all served in generous portions. The meal plus a pichet of inexpensive red wine costs about twelve Euros.

Café Marley... 93 rue de Rivoli, 1st Arr. Cour Napoleon – Louvre, Métro: Palais Royal, Tel: 01 49 26 06 60, Expensive.

Accessed through the Louvre's passage Richelieu, this arcaded café overlooks Pei's famed Pyramid. A sleek, and sophisticated crowd sips overpriced drinks (try the Chocolate Martini) served by an absurdly attractive staff. The food is nothing special, but Café Marley is all about the view.

Café de la Paix... 12 blvd des Capucines, 9th Arr. Métro; Opera, 12 bd des Capucines, 9th Arr., Tel: 01 40 07 36 36, Expensive.

Architect Charles Garnier designed this sumptuous café overlooking his more famous creation, the ornate Opera Garnier, designed for Emperor Napoleon III. A century ago, it was ground zero for Parisian café society. A former haunt of Josephine Baker, Oscar Wilde and the literary crowd, it is still a local institution. Staff, service, drinks and the traditional French cuisine are impeccable.

Sweet Seduction - *Le Chocolat:* Why does chocolate induce feelings of sexual arousal? Because chocolate affects key brain chemicals such as serotonin and phenyl ethylamine that heighten sensory perception, elevate mood and produce feelings of euphoria. Phenyl ethylamine is the same naturally occurring stimulant released in the brain when one falls in love. Scientists say that females are more susceptible to these effects and this explains why they appear to adore chocolate more than men.

The French government strictly regulates the production of chocolate, permitting the use of only pure cocoa butter, and allowing no fillers or additives. Most of the nation's gourmet chocolate producers actually use in excess of 80 percent pure cocoa butter before the other ingredients like caramel, nuts or liquor are added. This is the reason that French chocolates have such an intense flavor.

There are several master *chocolatiers* in Paris who maintain uncompromising world-class standards, producing fine chocolates of remarkable sophistication.

Jean-Paul Hévin... 231 rue Saint-Honoré, 1st Arr., Métro: Concorde, Tel: 01 55 35 35 96.

Hévin is considered by many chocolate connoisseurs to be the finest *artisan chocolatier* in Paris. His boutiques are an elegant temple for the purist. Hévin advises: "It must be enjoyed at room temperature, like a fine wine or a cake. You can recognize a fine chocolate by its dark, warm color and most of all, its fragrance. As soon as the box is opened, the aroma must be bold, pervasive, delicate, and insistent, all at the same time. It must suggest pleasure and whet the customer's appetite for the chocolate." The boutique's furnishings reflect taste, sophistication and perfection, combined with an atmosphere of elegance and comfort. This location includes an elegant tea room. There are four other locations throughout Paris.

La Maison du Chocolat... 225 rue du Faubourg St-Honoré, 8th Arr., Métro: Ternes, Tel: 01 42 27 39 44.

Robert Linxe opened his first signature "cocoa-color" boutique in 1977 and has remained in the top tier of Paris *chocolatiers* ever since. He is a compulsive perfectionist with tremendous attention to detail at every stage of production, purchasing only the highest quality cocoa beans from around the globe. He now has chic boutiques in New York and Tokyo with six locations in Paris.

Chocolat Chaud (Hot Chocolate)... Out and about on a cool, rainy day in Paris you may crave something warm, appealing and sinfully sweet? Actually, we were thinking of a delectable and restorative beverage, not a delectable and restorative romp.

Ladurée... 75 Avenue des Champs-Élysées, 8th Arr., Métro: George V, Tel: 01 40 75 08 75.

In 1862 Ladurée was the first luxurious tea salon opened in Paris. The spacious and elegant Champs-Élysées location is a combination restaurant, tea salon, pastry shop and ice creamerie. If possible, take a table on the more intimate second floor (the 2nd floor is called the *premiere étage* in France). Order the *chocolat chaud* (hot chocolate) and some of their signature macaroons. Be prepared for severe "chocolate shock" because this is not the same thin, milky concoction that you have been accustomed to back home. This is a near religious experience. The steaming *chocolat chaud* is served in a handsome, silver pitcher and when it is poured the dark, intense drink is almost thick enough to stand your spoon upright in the cup. Neither too bitter, or too sweet, this is truly cocoa ecstasy. A large portion of rich whipped cream is served along with a small pitcher of hot water to thin it down to your own taste. The original Ladurée is located at 16 rue Royale, 8th Arr., Métro: Madeleine.

Angélina... 226 rue de Rivoli, 1st Arr. Métro: Tuileries, Tel: 01 42 60 82 00.

Located near the Louvre, Angélina is renowned for refined pastries and desserts served in an historic tea salon. It was frequented by Coco Chanel and Marcel Proust, the famed French writer who was obsessed by their *madeleines* (a small French, cake-like cookie). Their most popular pastry is the decadent *Mont-Blanc,* a crunchy meringue base, piled with dense, sweet chestnut purée and unsweetened whipped cream. To complement this indulgence, order the *chocolat africain*, Angélina's rich, velvety and slightly sweet, hot chocolate, accompanied by a bowl of *crème Chantilly.*

Le Bar á Chocolat... 66, avenue des Champs Elysées, 8th Arr., (3rd floor) Métro: Georges V, Tel: 01 42 56 03 42.

An exotic salon with handsome, contemporary décor that features an exceptional selection of sinful chocolate drinks and other delights. The bar uses only imported Guanaja, Manjari and Caraibe cocoa. Popular with chic chocaholics. Open 9:00am to 7:30pm Mon to Sat.

Chapter Seven:

The Exuberant Parisian Nightlife

Chapter Seven:

"Nothing is so intolerable to man as being fully at rest, without a passion, without business, without entertainment, without care."

~ *Blaise Pascal* ~

Paris offers unlimited entertainment opportunities to visitors at every age and income level. Younger club goers flock to the numerous bars and high-tech dance club in the Bastille, Oberkampf, Ménilmontant and Canal St-Martin neighborhoods, while the stylish international crowd patronizes ultra-chic glam bars and exclusive clubs primarily in St-Honoré, Champs-Élysées and parts of St-Germain-des-Prés. With a very compact central city and a readily available transportation system (Metro), one can easily bar or club hop, exploring many options in a single evening.

Bars & Lounges

Le Fumoir... 6 rue de l'Amiral Coligny, 1st Arr., Métro: Louvre-Rivoli, Tel: 01 42 92 00 24, www.lefumoir.com.

Le Fumoir is a stylish upscale lounge/bar facing the East side of the Louvre. Patronized by a sophisticated, arty clientele, this deco bar is crowded during late afternoon and early evening. You can settle into the big leather club chairs in the lounge or enjoy dinner in the cozy candlelight of the library. Good food; half priced cocktails during Happy Hour; superb martinis; very popular for Sunday brunch. One of the author's favorite bars. Open daily 11:00 am–2:00 am.

Harry's New York Bar... 5 rue Daunou, 2nd Arr., Métro: Opéra, Tel: 01 42 61 71 14.

Harry's has remained a Parisian institution since opening on Thanksgiving Day in 1911. They serve expertly prepared cocktails to a mixed crowd of CEOs, post-theater attendees and college kids, in a clubby atmosphere of dark wood-paneled walls and red leather booths. The veteran bartenders may appear grumpy but are actually good natured. Harry's is renowned as the birthplace of the Bloody Mary (yes, they make an excellent one) and is, of course, another of Hemingway's many Paris haunts. There is a small piano bar downstairs. Hours: 10:30 am to 4:00 am daily.

Buddha Bar... 8 rue Boissy d'Anglas, 8th Arr. Métro: Concorde Tel: 01 53 05 90 00

The lounge/restaurant encompasses a huge space dominated by a colossal 20-foot Buddha. The burnt orange décor and highly eclectic background music provide a clubby atmosphere for the fashionable crowd. Asian-fusion cuisine is served in the restaurant. Buddha Bar may be too crowded on weekends so weekdays are recommended. Hours: 6:00 pm–2:00 am.

Le Dokhan's—Champagne Bar... Hotel Le Dokhans Sofitel, 117 rue de Lauriston, 16th Arr., Métro: Trocadéro, Tel: 01 53 65 66 99.

Le Dokhans is a romantic Champagne bar located in the Sofitel Hotel. Decorated in an elegant 18th century Baroque style, this is an ideal venue for a late evening drink by candle light. You may order by the flute or by the bottle from among the 50 varieties on offer (said to be the largest Champagne selection in the city). Wine and Champagne tastings are on offer every Thursday evening. There is a light dining menu for those who prefer a bit of *foie gras* or smoked salmon with their Champagne. Hours: Mon–Sat 8:00 am–2:00 am.

Le Rosebud... 11 bis rue Delambre, 6th Arr., Métro: Vavin, Tel: 01 43 35 38 54.

Looking for an authentic Parisian haunt patronized primarily by locals? Visit this atmospheric bar in the Montparnasse *quartier* frequented by writers, artists and journalists. Rosebud is friendlier, sees fewer tourists and attracts a more middle-aged clientele than many of the trendy haunts. Hours: 7:00 pm–2:00 am daily.

La Mezzanine de l'Alcazar... 62 Rue Mazarine, 6th Arr., Métro: Odéon, Tel: 01 55 42 22 00.

The mezzanine bar of the Alcazar Restaurant has the look of a sleek Manhattan lounge set in St-Germain-des-Prés. The high-tech, airy look is typical of British restaurateur Sir Terence Conran. Sit in a cozy armchair, have a cocktail and look out over the fashionable ground-floor restaurant below. If you want to dance, the trendy WAGG Club is below the restaurant. Fashionable crowd - great sushi rolls - eclectic atmosphere. Live DJ Wed to Sat 8:00 pm–2:00 am.

Uber-Chic Bars... The exclusive bars & lounges in this section are among the most fashionable in Europe, presenting a sophisticated view of Parisian life at its most glamorous. These refined (and expensive) venues always require appropriate dress (i.e., ultra stylish).

Black Calvados (BC)... 40 avenue Pierre 1 de Serbie, Métro: Franklin D. Roosevelt, Tel: 01 45 44 73 73, www.bc-paris.fr

Tucked away on a side street not far from the Hotel George V, this upscale lounge/bar/club caters to a glamorous international clientele. Black, high gloss, lacquered walls, smoked mirrors and subtle lighting touches provide a unique contemporary feel. The boisterous dance floor is packed with attractive, urbane patrons. Restaurant on ground level with the club below. Like every club du jour the doormen are discriminating.

Bar du Hotel Costes... Hotel Costes, 239 rue Saint-Honore, 1st Arr., Métro: Concorde, Tel: 01 42 44 50 00

The bar and lounge at the Hotel Costes continues to be a favorite among fashionistas, pouty models and international celebrities. Designed in a stunningly original Italian Baroque style, the lounge is a maze of candlelit rooms furnished with comfortable velvet couches. A breathtakingly attractive staff provides the customary service with attitude. The restaurant is set on a sumptuous terrace in the center of the hotel's courtyard. Good for late night cocktails or dinner—do not go underdressed—over-crowded on weekends. Hours: 7:00 pm–2:00 am.

The Bar Hemingway... Hotel Ritz, 15 place Vendôme, 1st Arr., Métro: Opéra, Tel: 01 43 16 30 30

The discreet charm of the place Vendôme. The Hemingway Bar, at the very back of the Hotel Ritz, presents an intimate, clubby atmosphere that pulls their loyal clientele back again and again. The charismatic manager and head barman, Colin Field, has presided in this domain for over 14 years and is world famous, having been the subject of numerous articles in global business and travel publications ("World's Greatest Bartender" - Forbes). His amazing expertise in preparing just the right drink for the mood or occasion is unparalleled. One of his signature cocktails is the Picasso Martini, made with Tanqueray No. Ten (served at exactly 18.4°C) and a miniature frozen cube of Noilly Pratt vermouth. Another favorite is the French 75, a heady mix of *Champagne,* gin and lemon juice (invented during World War I). In a chivalrous gesture, every lady receives a rose draped over the edge of her drink glass.

The bar was named after the indomitable Ernest Hemingway, who with a small group of GI's—famously liberated the Hotel Ritz on August 25th, 1944. He was serving as a war correspondent for *Collier's* magazine at the time and having raced ahead of the invading army in his jeep was one of the first Allies to enter the Paris. After capturing a couple of elderly German hotel staff doing laundry in the basement, he raided the wine cellar, then got thoroughly drunk in the bar, forever memorializing the American fighting (and journalistic) spirit. The number of bars around the globe that claim "Hemingway drank here" are legion but this, my friend, is the genuine article.

The diminutive bar is decorated with warm wood paneling, and features photos and memorabilia of the great writer. It is a traditional rendezvous for chic singles and Parisian power couples. Obviously, it is also very popular with Americans and literary types. Age group: 25 to 50. The small size, comfortable configuration and intimate atmosphere make this an ideal spot to meet, and mix with cosmopolitan prospects. The *Times* called the Bar Hemingway "the best kept secret in Paris." Hours: 6:00 pm–2:00 am; closed Sun and Mon. Expensive. Colin is known to keep the bar open "after hours" if circumstances dictate.

On the memorable day that the author of this guide moved to and began a new life in Paris, he celebrated with an uninhibited, all-night bash at the Bar Hemingway. He has remained a faithful patron of this splendid Parisian establishment ever since.

Le Bar du Plaza Athénée

Hotel Plaza Athénée... 25 avenue Montaigne, 8th Arr., Métro: Alma-Marceau, Tel: 01 53 67 65 00

Le Bar at the luxury Hotel Plaza Athénée is a contrast of contemporary and classic in a glamorous "see and be seen" environment. The bar's daring design and mood lighting create a sensual ambiance. The space is divided into two areas, one focused around the long, sand-blasted glass bar illuminated in electric blue, and the other around comfortable leather armchairs and low bar tables positioned for intimate conversation.

Le Bar serves various signature drinks such as the Fashion Ice, a translucent, alcoholic ice pop in flavors Bellini yellow and apple green. Also try the Champagne mojito and their heavenly ice cream based cocktails. Caters to a very elegant and polished clientele so wear your *haute couture*—crowded on weekends. Hours: 6:00 pm–2:00 am daily.

Kong... 1 rue du Pont Neuf, 1st Arr., Métro: Pont Neuf, Tel: 01 40 39 09 00

A highly stylized bar/restaurant/club by designer Philippe Starck, Kong is situated on the 5th and 6th floors of the LVMH building above the Kenzo store. Audaciously ultra modern with fluorescent staircases, acrylic rocking chairs and huge plasma screens, it is patronized by a moneyed and trendy crowd. The restaurant, serving Asian fare, on the top floor features a glass roof and walls with a jaw-dropping view of the river and Pont Neuf. A DJ spins tunes for dancing in the bar.

The Thursday night soirées are highly recommended or try dinner at sunset for the views. Hours: Open 7 days a week until 2:30 am.

Dance Clubs... You will find hundreds of nightspots, bursting with energy, where Parisians and visitors gather to dance the night away. Whether you prefer house, techno, salsa, classic rock or swing, you will find the appropriate venue somewhere in Paris. Serious club devotees (most in their 20s and early 30s) meet earlier in the evening at a café or DJ bar, have a late dinner, then proceed to the club. Most dance clubs open their doors around midnight, but Parisians wouldn't think of arriving before 1:30 or 2:00am when things begin to get lively. The clubs stay open until dawn. For regulars, Thursdays have actually become one of the major party nights because fewer attendees flow in from the suburbs. Most venues sponsor "club nights" explained below. Remember that the Métro is closed between 1:00 and 5:30 am except Saturday when it runs until 2:30 am. While this is only a small selection of the available clubs, it represents some of the most popular:

Nouveau Casino... 109 rue Oberkampf, 11th Arr., Métro: Parmentier, Tel: 01 43 57 57 40

This massive dance club in the lively Oberkampf area sports an unusual bar with an iceberg theme (reasonable drink prices) and an edgy, post rock music selection. Club nights are Wed to Sat with live concerts nightly between 8:00 pm and 1:00 am and dancing till dawn. Music: techno, house, electro.

Mix Club... 24 rue de l'Arrivée, 15th Arr., Métro: Montparnasse-Bienvenüe, Tel: 01 56 80 37 37

An enormous club (capacity of 1,500) situated in an attractive space featuring high ceilings, three balconies and a very large dance floor. Mix Club has a glamorous VIP area, top of the line DJs, a state of the art sound system and impressive lighting effects. The club exudes great energy. Open Wed to Sat: 11:00 pm–6:00 am, Sun: 5:00 pm–1:00 am. Music: house. While the club itself is quite impressive, it is located in the hideous Montparnasse Tower, an architectural abomination built in the 1960s despite the city's height controls. It remains a 56-story wart on the lovely face of low-rise Paris.

Le Triptyque... 142 rue Montmartre, 2nd Arr., Métro: Grands Boulevards, Tel: 01 40 28 05 55

A popular club, near the Bourse, patronized by an eclectic international crowd. Dance in the concert hall where live bands alternate with DJ nights, or relax with friends in the comfortable lounge. Relatively inexpensive drinks—good staff attitude—a good time. Open Wed: 10:30 pm–6:00 am; Thurs to Sun: 11:00 pm–6:00 am. Music: electro.

Rex Club... 5 boulevard Poissonnière, 2nd Arr., Métro: Bonne-Nouvelle, Tel: 01 40 28 95 62

The Rex is considered to be Paris's top techno club. If you like it intensely loud, sweaty, and often chemically enhanced this is the place for you. A mind numbing sound system, younger crowd, and rather easy to get in. Open Wed to Sat: 11:30 pm–dawn.

Batofar... Quai Francois-Mauriac, 13th Arr., Métro: Quai de la Gare, Tel: 01 56 29 10 20

The club is situated on a huge, crimson colored, lighthouse boat anchored on the Seine and is one of the all-night favorites of clubbers in their 20s and 30s. Batofar provides a mix of musical styles and a laid-back atmosphere. Stay and watch the sunrise at the "after-parties" held two Sundays a month. In good weather the crowd extends out onto the adjacent quai. Three bars, a 1000 sq ft dance floor and restaurant. Open Mon to Sat: 11:00 pm–6:00 am. Closed November to March.

Cithéa... 114, rue Oberkampf, 11th Arr., Métro: Parmentier, Tel: 01 40 21 70 95

If you a looking for a club that is a bit more manageable in size, Cithéa serves as a cozy alternative, with a small dance floor and music ranging from electro to Latin to acid jazz. This club attracts a young crowd (no sneakers/trainers). Open Tues to Thurs 10:00 pm–5:30 am; Fri & Sat 10:00 pm–6:30 am. Sat is ultra crowded.

Le Cab (Cabaret)... 2 place du Palais Royal, 1st Arr., Métro: Palais Royal–Musée du Louvre, Tel: 01 58 62 56 25

An exclusive, modern club/lounge/restaurant with an intimate atmosphere despite its 1,000-square-meter size. Models and upscale tourists lounge in private alcoves and dance to house, hip hop and R&B spun by DJs. The age group ranges from 20 to 45. Le Cab's fine restaurant is by reservation only. Located next to the Palais Royal. Fri nights are particularly hot. Open Mon to Sat 9:00 pm–6:00 am.

Flèche d'Or... 102 bis, rue de Bagnolet, 20th Arr., Métro: Porte de Bagnolet, Tel: 01 44 64 01 02

An abandoned railway station *(Gare de Charonne)* was renovated to create this bar, club, restaurant and free concert venue (9:00pm nightly) that serves as a nightspot for younger Parisians. Open Mon & Sun: 8:00 pm–2:00 am; Wed to Sat: 8:00 pm–5:00 am. Restaurant is open 8:00pm–midnight, with Sun brunch noon–5:00 pm. Prices are very reasonable.

Le Paris Paris... 5 ave de l'Opéra, 1st Arr., Paris Métro: Pyramides, Tel: 01 42 60 64 45

An intimate club (capacity 300) opened by the owners of the very successful Le Baron. Popular with the art and fashion set, this nightspot is jammed with fabulous, very thin 20-somethings dancing to an eclectic mix of electro, and rock. Strict door policy. Open daily 10:00 pm–5:00 am.

Les Bains Douche... 7 rue du Bourg-l'Abbé, 3rd Arr., Métro: Étienne Marcel, Tel: 01 48 87 01 80

A cool, late-night club with a mythic reputation. It occupies a former Turkish bathhouse and has recently been renovated, and equipped with a cutting edge sound and light system. Les Bains has been an institution in Paris for many years and it still draws a well-heeled crowd, but its new door policy has made it more accessible. Clubbers can easily bypass the bouncers by making reservations in the Thai restaurant upstairs. For the intrepid, who dance until dawn, there is an "After Party" from 6:00 am to noon. Music: house, rock, disco. Open Wed to Sun 11:00 pm–6:00 am.

Last Tango in Paris

La Coupole (Retro Dance Hall)... 102 bd du Montparnasse, 14th Arr., Métro: Vavin, Tel: 01 43 27 56 00

Dancing cheek to cheek—what a concept! Retro dancing on Friday and Saturday nights. Waltzing to a full orchestra, romantic couples representing every age group crowd the ballroom below the famous brasserie. Occasional Salsa nights – check the schedule. Popular tea dances are held on Sun at 3:00 pm.

Uber-Chic Clubs - Clubbing with Attitude...

Paris is host to a number of stylish, upscale clubs that attract an elite international clientele. These cosmopolitan nightspots are major "see and be seen" territory. The clubs listed have an exceptionally selective door policy, so definitely dress to impress, in your designer wear. One way to circumvent the doorman's disdain is to simply reserve a table for dinner, as most of these clubs have a restaurant.

Club Le Baron... 6 avenue Marceau, 8th Arr., Métro: Alma-Marceau, Tel: 01 47 20 03 01 www.clublebaron.com

Currently the most elite dance venue in the city; Le Baron is located in a former, brothel that has retained its sensuous red interior, black ceiling, plush velvet couches and soft interior lighting. This intimate club has a capacity of only 150 so there is a particularly challenging door policy that favors socialites, fashionistas and celebrities, but it is still possible to get in. A good size dance floor, friendly staff and some of the best DJs in Europe make it a very elegant winner. Featuring live bands Sun through Wed. Open daily 10:00 pm–5:00 am.

L'Etoile... 12 rue de Presbourg, 16th Arr., Métro: Charles de Gaulle-Étoile, Tel: 01 45 00 78 70, www.letoileparis.com

A beautiful club/bar/restaurant for beautiful people situated in a private mansion with a view of the Arc de Triomphe. This luxurious club hosts many glamorous events including celebrity birthday parties and *haute couture* shows. L'Etoile features high ceilings, parquet floors, a splendid restaurant (with an innovative menu), plush lounge bar and a romantic terrace-garden. The dance floor is full of *Parisiennes* in their best, so mosey down to avenue Montaigne, buy your lady an absurdly expensive designer dress and fetch her up to L'Etoile.

She will be forever grateful. Open Mon to Sun noon–1:30 pm and 8:00 pm–12:30 am.

Soirées... A soirée is an "evening party," and a *club soirée* (also known as "club night") is a "party" hosted by a club or other venue, advertised in advance. Club *soirées* usually feature a special theme, a top musical group or a well-known DJ and *admission is limited to those who register in advance* for the event. All of the top rated clubs in Paris host a soirée on a given night and that night (most often a weekday) becomes the big event of the week for that club. Registering for a soirée is an ideal way to avoid waiting in line at the club of your choice. You pay the admission fee in advance and your name is placed on the guest list held by the doorman. It is possible to register online and be placed on the list or you can call the club directly. For some soirées you may also be required to print an invitation. Several web sites list the complete schedule of Paris soirée dates in English and French. These sites are:

- ParisInfo: http://en.parisinfo.com (What's On > Paris at Night > Clubbing > Parties)
- Cityvox: www.eng.cityvox.fr/guide_paris/CityHome
- Nightfloor: www.nightfloor.com

VIP Soirées... VIP *soirées* are those held at the pre-eminent, up-market clubs including: L'Etoile, La Maison Blanche, Le VIP Room, La Milliardaire, and Le Ritz Club among others. The schedule for most of these high-caliber soirées are listed on one of these three *French-language only* web sites: workinzecity.org, amiral-prod.com and lestzars.com (to translate their content use http://translate.google.com/translate_t). These three public relations firms provide special event planning services for a small number of elite clubs in the city. The PR firms essentially function as the club's "gatekeeper" by screening potential guests. Although they are highly selective, with a bit of *savoir-faire* you can secure an invitation to one of these chic events.

VIP soirées are periodically held at the historic Maxim's Restaurant owned by designer Pierre Cardin. The events, which take place in the elegant Belle-Époque reception rooms above the restaurant, are exclusive all-night affairs for approximately 800 "invited" guests. Attendees are largely from the smart, Parisian set. Maxim's, 3 rue Royale, 8th Arr., Métro: La Madeleine. Tel: 01 42 65 27 94. For information and a schedule of events see "Maxim Nights" at www.maxims-de-paris.com or email maxinsclubinternational@maxims-de-paris.com.

Jazz Clubs...

Duc des Lombards... 42 rue des Lombards, 1st Arr., Métro: Châtelet–Les Halles, Tel: 01 42 33 22 88

Considered one of the top jazz venues in Paris for over two decades, the club features French and international jazz greats. This is one of the few jazz clubs that permit you to reserve a table in advance. Concerts at 9:30 pm Mon to Sat.

Le Slow Club... 130 rue de Rivoli, 1st Arr., Métro: Châtelet, Tel: 01 42 33 84 30

The medieval ceiling vaults of this old banana warehouse provide a distinctive atmosphere and superb acoustics. Big Band, Dixieland, and rock 'n' roll. An old Miles Davis haunt. Open Tues to Thurs 10:00 pm–3:00 am. Fri & Sat till 4:00 am. Live music and dancing.

Le Sunset... 60 rue des Lombards, 1st Arr., Métro: Châtelet, Tel: 01 40 26 46 60

This club is for the very serious jazz enthusiast. Patrons don't talk or party, they just listen in rapt silence. There are two separate venues at *Le Sunside;* the ground floor is home to traditional jazz and *Le Sunset* located down in the cellar is oriented toward electronic jazz. This is a comfortable and relaxed environment where musicians come to jam after their other gigs. There is a mixed, mostly upscale crowd representing every age group. Open every day from 9:30 pm to 4:00 am except Sun.

Wine Bars...

Wine is one of life's seductive pleasures and pleasant wine bars are a fixture in every quarter of the city. With their superior selection and fine cuisine, they have emerged as a competitor to traditional cafés and bistros. Many offer a warm, friendly atmosphere, special regional wine tastings and special events celebrating the annual harvest. All wine bars appear to be closed on Sunday.

Willi's Wine Bar... 13 Rue de Petits Champs, 2nd Arr., Métro: Palais Royal–Musée du Louvre, Tel: 01 42 61 05 09

Opened in 1980 and owned by Englishman Mark Williamson, Willi's has become a popular haunt of British and

American expats and visitors. The atmosphere is friendly, and a vast selection is available by the glass or bottle. During lunch, the long polished oak bar is crowded with stockbrokers and lawyers from the surrounding financial district. A cozy dining room serves reasonably priced, seasonal cuisine in the Mediterranean style. Stop in for a mid-afternoon break and ask the barman to serve a crisp Rhône white accompanied by a smooth French cheese. Open: Lunch Wed to Sat 11:30 am–4:30 pm; Dinner Sun to Thurs 5:00 pm–9:00 pm; Fri & Sat 5:00 pm–10:00 pm.

Taverne Heni IV... 13 place du Pont Neuf, 1st Arr., Métro: Pont Neuf, Tel: 01 43 54 27 90

Taverne Henri IV is known as much for its picturesque location as it is for its wines. Located on the Pont Neuf, right at the tip of the Ile de la Cité, this 50-year-old establishment with rustic furnishings and a dark clubby atmosphere, is also justly famous for its simple, hearty fare. Try the *foie gras,* the pungent cheeses, goose *rillettes, saucisson* (sausage), wild boar pâté or the eggs baked with blue cheese and ham. The wine is purchased directly from the vintner and bottled on the premises by the proprietor. The selection includes a wide array of Burgogne, Bordeaux, Beaujolais, Sauternes and various wines from the Loire Valley which are reasonably priced by the glass. Open Mon to Fri 11:30 am–10:00 pm; Sat 11:30 am–3:00 pm; closed Sun.

l'Ecluse... 15 place de la Madeleine, 8th Arr., Métro: Madeleine, Tel: 01 42 65 34 69, www.leclusebaravin.com/us

A warm and welcoming establishment that specializes in minor and major Bordeaux vintages from Graves to Margaux to Pauillac, including such greats as Château Pétrus '79 and Chateau Latour '95. Thirty of the forty-five wines available are sold by the glass. L'Ecluse Madeleine (one of six locations in Paris) features a glass-roofed courtyard and a charming stone cellar. The bistro-style menu of seasonal specialties includes steak tartare, *foie gras,* Serrano ham, fillet of duck, Norwegian smoked salmon and various cheeses. The staff will gladly suggest a wine to accompany your meal including dessert. Open 11:30 am–1:00 am daily except Sun.

Erotic Cabarets & Nightclubs... The best of the extravagant grand cabarets have been entertaining visitors since the 19th century. Many feel that they have not properly experienced Paris until they have taken in one of these *grands spectacles* complete with feathers, sequins and risqué revues. All of the major venues offer a dinner show. Reservations are obligatory.

Le Moulin Rouge... 82 boulevard de Clichy, 18th Arr., Métro: Blanche, Tel: 01 53 09 82 82 Show times: Daily dinner-show 7:00 pm, shows at 9:00 and 11:00 pm.

During the Universal Exhibition of 1889, a wild and wanton air of frivolity burst over the bohemian quarter of *Montmartre* as high-society Parisians were drawn to the music-halls by bawdy entertainment and seductive courtesans. High-kicking dancers lifted their ruffled skirts, showing off their shapely legs and often their genitalia to the delight of the rapturous crowd. Perhaps the most memorable patron of the Le Moulin Rouge was Henri de Toulouse-Lautrec, who captured the joyful essence of the period in his vivid paintings and prints. Immortalized in literature and film, Le Moulin Rouge remains a highly entertaining venue for adult visitors from around the world. Their glittering revues, sumptuous sets and brilliant choreography celebrate the provocative essence of Belle Époque Paris.

Lido de Paris... 116 bis avenue Des Champs-Élysées, 8th Arr., Métro: George V, Tel: 01 40 76 56 10, Show times: Daily dinner-show 8:00 pm, shows at 9:30 pm and midnight, matinee at 1:00 pm.

The Lido de Paris, located on the avenue de Champs-Élysées, presents *grand revues* in one of the largest theatres in Europe. Lido shows are celebrated for their technical wizardry, special effects and of course, the stunningly, beautiful girls. The Lido features a dinner menu styled in collaboration with famous French chef Paul Bocuse.

Folies Bergeres... 32 rue Richter, 9th Arr., Métro: Cadet, Tel: 01 44 79 98 98, Show times: Daily dinner-show 7:00 pm, show at 9:15 pm.

Opened in 1869, this cabaret has seen great vaudeville performers such as Will Rogers, Maurice Chevalier, the Marx Brothers and Charlie Chaplin. In the 20's the American exotic dancer Josephine Baker wowed Parisian audiences while wearing little more than a banana skirt. The grand music-hall tradition continues today with adaptations of Broadway musicals and scantily clad dancers.

Le Paradis Latin... 28 rue du Cardinal-Lemoine, 5th Arr. Métro: Cardinal-Lemoine, Tel: 01 43 25 28 28, Show times: Dinner-show 8:00 pm Wed to Mon., show 9:30 & 11:15 pm.

Le Paradis Latin, the only "music hall" situated on the Left Bank is considered the Grand Dame of the Paris cabarets. It was here that Yvette Guilbert emerged as the first International French star during the Universal Exhibition of 1889. The highest cabaret traditions established during that period continue today with beautiful girls, stylish costumes, and a dazzling show.

Intimate Cabarets

Crazy Horse Saloon... 12 Avenue George V, 8th Arr., Métro: Alma-Marceau, Tel: 01 47 23 32 32, Show times: Sun to Fri 8:30 and 11:00 pm, Sat 7:30, 9:45 and 11:00 pm.

Founded by Alain Bernardin in 1951, this internationally famous Parisian landmark is known to have breathtakingly beautiful girls. With sensational choreography, the innovative show has some of most talented dancers in show business. A one of a kind performance.

Au Lapin Agile... 22 rue des Saules, 18th Arr., Métro: Lamarck-Caulaincourt, Tel: 01 46 06 85 87, Show times: Tues to Sun 9:00 pm to 2:00 am.

A Parisian classic located in colorful Montmartre. This popular little club is the oldest cabaret in Paris and traditionally attracted the best-known writers, painters and artists of the period. Picasso once paid his bill with a painting and the walls are covered with bohemian memorabilia. It offers a very "traditional" evening of French love ballads, folk tunes and quaint entertainment in a venue dating from 1860.

Chez Michou... 80 rue des Martyrs, 18th Arr., Métro: Pigalle, Tel: 01 46 06 16 04, Show times: 11:00 pm daily

A famous and very extravagant drag show. The club is owned and operated by the flamboyant impresario Michou. A talented collection of cross-dressing performers imitate well-known international singers and entertainers. Michou remains the best "boys as girls" club in the city.

Chapter Eight:
The Paris Day Spa–Indulgent Care of the Body

"In Paris, all of
the senses are sated.
There is pleasure
for the mind,
the body, the palate."

~ Anonymous ~

Chapter Eight:

From ancient times, bathing in the thermal waters bubbling up from deep in the earth has been seen as a pleasurable and purifying ritual associated with relaxation, good health and regeneration. These traditions persist today at selected day spas throughout the city. Enjoy the luxury of curative baths, aroma or massage therapy and nurturing, world-renowned French skin, body and anti-aging treatments.

Care of the skin has long been a crucial part of every French woman's beauty regimen. As young girls, they learn the rituals of personal grooming from their mothers with particular attention paid to the skin. It is not unusual for girls in their early teens to begin receiving facials and other beauty care treatments. This single-minded dedication at a young age pays enormous dividends at age 40 or 50, with nearly perfect, glowing skin, allowing the mature women to manage with minimal makeup.

The wide range of sophisticated body care treatments available at Paris spas include facials, body wraps, many styles of massage, skin detoxification, dermabrasion, salt scrubs, mud baths, anti-cellulite treatments, waxing, makeup, hair care, manicures, pedicures and electrolysis.

Of course, men require relaxation and physical rejuvenation just as much as the ladies. Males constitute almost 50 percent of the Paris day spa clientele and many spas offer special packages for couples.

Spa—Four Seasons Hotel—Georges V... 31 avenue George V, 8th Arr., Métro: Georges V, Tel: 01 49 52 70 00, www.fourseasons.com/paris/spa.html

Ranked as one of the finest spas in France by *Travel and Leisure Magazine,* this luxurious retreat offers an extensive array of skin, body and aromatherapy treatments. The facility includes saunas, steam baths and a lovely pool surrounded by *trompe l'oeil* gardens. Among their signature offerings is the "Wonder Bust" seaweed treatment that strengthens the chest's web of tissue, provides immediate lift to the breasts and tone to the cleavage, resulting in a more seductive décolleté. Also for a unique (and delicious) experience try the full body chocolate wrap. Finally there is the Romantic Couple's Massage—the classic, full-body Swedish massage for you and your partner, in a private room with two therapists.

Cinq Mondes... 6 square Opéra Louis Jouvet, 8th Arr., Métro: Opéra, Tel: 01 42 66 00 60

Exotic, oriental treatments, baths and Ayurvedic massage offered in a serene and luxurious environment. Cinq Monde features Japanese o-furo baths strewn with flower petals and a relaxing Turkish bath (hammam).

Hotel Meurice Day Spa... 228 rue de Rivoli, 1st Arr., Tel: 01 44 58 10 10, Métro: Tuileries, www.meuricehotel.com/fitness_spa/espace.html

Three thousand square feet of comfort dedicated to well-being, balance and Gallic-style pampering. Based on *vinotherapie,* the use of beauty products from grapes—Grand Cru facial, Vinolift treatment, Merlot body wrap, and Crushed Cabernet Scrub for an invigorating organic restorative.

Lancôme Institut... 29 rue du Faubourg Saint-Honore, 8th Arr., Tel: 01 42 65 30 74, Métro: Concorde

Lancôme established the institute to provide their clients with comprehensive services such as skin treatment and exclusive therapeutic massage techniques to stimulate cutaneous microcirculation. Body resculpting reduces the appearance of cellulite while increasing skin tone and firmness. Also shop for an exceptional variety of skincare, makeup and fragrance products often unavailable in stores back home. One of France's premier brands, Lancôme has been producing cosmetic products for more than 66 years.

Anne Sémonin Spa... Hotel Le Bristol, 112 rue Faubourg, St. Honore, 8th Arr., Métro: Miromesnil, Tel: 01 42 66 24 22

The in-house spa of the Bristol Hotel is famous for its extraordinary standards of service set in a luxurious environment. Treatments for men and women include: phyto-aromatic facials, Dead-Sea salt body-scrub, as well as a highly restorative jet lag treatment. Massages include: Ayurvedic, Thai and Shiatsu.

Spa at Royal Monceau... Hotel Royal Monceau 37 Avenue Hoche, 8th Arr., Tel: 01 42 99 88 00, Métro: Charles de Gaulle–Étoile, www.royalmonceau.com

The Thermes and Spa at Royal Monceau are a promise of relaxation and enhancement with opportunities for slimming and toning. Extensive facilities include swimming pool, hammam, sauna, gymnasium, yoga, balneotherapy treatments. Beauty center with hair salon and facials. The intimate *Restaurant des Thermes* overlooks the swimming pool.

Le 32 Montorgueil Spa Nuxe... 32 rue Montorgueil, 1st Arr., Métro: Les Halles, Tel: 01 55 80 71 40

This fashionable spa is housed in the ancient vaulted cellars of a former 12th-century wine warehouse. Created by cosmetologist Aliza Jabès, Nuxe offers a full range of treatments, massages and anti-aging cures. John Nollet, one of the hottest hairstylists in Paris, styles for Spa Nuxe.

Les Bains du Marais... 31-33 rue des Blancs Monteaux, 4th Arr., Tel: 01 44 61 02 02, Métro: Rambuteau, www.lesbainsdumarais.com/bdm_site.html

An elegant spa located in the Marais, offering a comprehensive range of services including massages, facials, hair salon, manicures, pedicures, and waxing. The harmonious honey-colored stone throughout the facility creates a warm and relaxing environment. Hammam, sauna and restaurant.

Le Quickie Massage... Walk-in customers may enjoy a "quickie" at one of the city's massage cafés.

No Stress Café... 2 place Gustave Toudouze, 9th Arr., Métro: St Georges, Tel: 01 48 78 00 27

A café/restaurant that offers a 10 minute Japanese shiatsu massage for only €10.

Massage Café... 181 rue Saint-Martin, 3rd Arr., Métro: Châtelet, Tel: 01 48 04 05 53

An "a la carte" massage bar offering massage and drink of choice for a mere €17.

Hair & Beauty

Autour de Christophe Robin... 9 rue Guénégaud, 6th Arr., Métro: Mabillon, Tel: 01 42 60 99 15

Robin is reputed to be the most talented colorist in France. "The right color is one that shows a woman's personal style and beauty off to their best advantage. I like to hear people say she's a beautiful woman, not her hair color is beautiful," says

Robin. He does Catherine Deneuve's blond locks. Makeup, manicures, pedicures—this is the total makeover for women and men, all under one roof.

John Nollet... 32 rue Montorgueil, 1st Arr., Métro: Les Halles, Tel: 01 55 80 71 40

One of the hottest hair stylists in Paris, Nollet cuts the hair of Monica Bellucci, Emmanuelle Béart, Vanessa Paradis and Audrey Tautou.

"All the reasonings
of men are not worth
one sentiment
of women."

~ *Voltaire* ~

Chapter Nine:
Eclectic Adventures, Diversions & Frivolous Amusements

Paris offers an unrivalled range of amusing diversions and revelries that often remain undiscovered by visitors. These social gatherings provide a unique opportunity to mix with long-time American, British and other expatriates as well as Parisians.

Pique-Nique – Pont des Arts... The splendid pedestrian bridge over the Seine known as the Pont des Arts is a very popular location for picnics during the warm weather months drawing friendly groups of both locals and visitors. Built in 1802, the classic, arched, metal bridge with a wooden-deck and benches, stretches from the Louvre (on the Right Bank) to the Institut de France (on the Left Bank).

Visit the local shops to purchase the necessary wine, cheese, bread and pâte for a *pique-nique en plein air* (in the open air) and join the festive atmosphere that includes people from every nation. In mid-summer, the sun does not set in Paris until almost 10:00 pm providing stunning views of the grand architecture crowding the banks of the Seine.

In 1999, Edward Flaherty, a well-known American film-maker who has lived in Paris for 33 years, organized a weekly picnic on the Pont that provided a place for local expatriates and Parisians to meet, socialize and network. The event was even broadcast live on French television. The tradition caught on and the celebration continues today.

Métro: Louvre – Rivoli

Biking in the Park... Spend a glorious and invigorating day biking across the residential portion of west-side Paris into and through the pastoral Bois de Boulogne. We have selected this particular route through the fashionable 16th Arrondissement because it is relatively safe (fairly low in vehicular traffic) and the residential architecture along the way is grand. You will need a Paris map (we recommend one called *Paris Pratique,* the blue-covered, pocket-sized map book can be found at any news kiosk for a couple of Euros). We also recommend Fat Tire Bike Tours for rentals because their big-tired bikes do particularly well on the cobblestone streets, and the friendly, American-owned management team is very helpful. After renting bikes at their shop a couple of blocks east of the Eiffel Tower, ride over to blvd de Grenelle and follow it toward the river Seine crossing over the Pont de Bir Hakeim. Turn left on rue Raynouard. Follow rue Raynourd south to rue Ranleigh, turn right and it is a straight shot to the Bois de Boulogne. Once you are in the park, follow your own routes along the various park trails using the map book. We like the very scenic route around the two lakes (Lac Superior and Lac Inferieur). Take a break for lunch on the sun-drenched terrace at the very rustic Chalet des Iles restaurant (see restaurant chapter for details) on an island on Lac Inferieur. However, be sure to make reservations in advance. Return by the same route or find your own way back to Fat Tire Bike Tours using the map book.

Should you not be confident enough to venture out on your own, Fat Tire offers both "escorted" bike and Segway tours.

24, rue Edgar Faure, 15th Arr., Métro: Dupleix, Tel: 01 56 58 10 54, www.fattirebiketoursparis.com

As an alternative you can rent a bike at any of the 750 Velib stations (automated bike rental stations) throughout the city and conveniently drop it off at any other station without having to return to your point of departure.

Paris Plage... Every summer the City of Paris converts a two-mile stretch of the Right Bank quai of the River Seine into "Paris Plage" (Paris beach) with 2000 tons of fine sand, potted palm trees, sun-loungers and even a 28-meter swimming pool—all for the enjoyment and relaxation of residents and visitors. The entire project lasts until September then disappears for the winter. This highly innovative project has received worldwide publicity and is crowded everyday with thankful sun worshipers in skimpy bikinis and tank suits. "Paris Plage" stretches from east of the Pont Sully to the west of the Pont Neuf.

Cinema... This may be the last refuge of the die-hard cinephile. As independent art house theaters disappear from cities around the globe, they continue to flourish in Paris. If you are accustomed to seeing only mainstream commercial films at your local mall megaplex, some of these Parisian venues will renew your love affair with the international independent film medium.

There are a mind-boggling 300 titles playing week in and week out at various theaters featuring classic and obscure works from American film noir to Japanese New Wave to German Expressionism. *Pariscope* magazine (for half a Euro) and available at any news kiosk, lists all show times and indicates if the film is shown in its original language version subtitled in French (VO) or French language-dubbed versions (VF). There are numerous films screening in English. Schedules are also online at www.allocine.fr.

Certain aspects of the French film-going experience that are particularly enjoyable: 1) no one talks during the film; 2) cell phones are jammed in all French movie houses; and 3) they actually still have uniformed ushers (remember those?) who can show you to your seat.

Among notable movie palaces in Paris are the *Panthéon* at 13 rue Victor-Cousin in the 5th Arr. Built in 1907, it is the oldest movie house in Paris and was the first to show films in English. And there is *La Pagode*, a highly atmospheric theater originally built in 1931. It is located at 57 rue de Babylone, 7th Arr. *Le Grand Rex*, on blvd Poissonnière in the 10th Arr. The theater is a national historical monument with three levels of seats, featuring Art Deco decor and original wall murals.

Romantic Cinema

Under the Stars... Enjoy free films at the *Festival de en Plein Air* (Festival of in the open air). Funded by the City of Paris, the screenings take place nightly on a large manicured lawn in the Parc de la Villette. So find a date, a bottle of wine, prepare a *pique-nique* and bring your blanket. Films are screened in their original language and the program includes such classics as Hitchcock's *The Birds*, Truffaut's *L'Enfant Sauvage,* contemporary films such as Woody Allen's *Match Point* and Sophia Coppola's *Marie-Antoinette.* Lawn chairs and blankets are available for rental at the site.

Parc de la Villette, 19th Arr., Métro: Porte de Pantin, Tel: 01 40 03 75 75, www.villette.com/us/mainprog.htm

MK2 Bibliothèque ... When the lights go down at the MK2 Bibliothèque , lovers are able to snuggle up in the theater's cozy and comfortable two-seater armchairs. The arm rest between seats flips up to create a love seat.

128–168 ave de France, 13th Arr., Métro: Bibliothèque François Mitterrand Tel: 0 892 69 84 84 (#01)

Film Rouge... For film lovers this theater (a former music hall) offers an unusual amenity – an old staircase leads up to a cozy wine bar tucked neatly into the area above and behind the screen. The wine bar has a decent selection and serves light soups and salads. All in all, a respectable alternative to popcorn and a Coke.

7 ave de Clichy, 17th Arr., Métro: Place de Clichy, Tel: 01 53 42 40 00

Archive & Library... The famous *Cinémathèque Française* hosts the largest archive of films, movie documents, and film-related objects in the world. Founded in the 1930s by Henri Langlois, an ardent cineaste, the institution schedules frequent retrospectives and thematic programming, as well as films on demand from their massive library. Wish to see a rare film? Ask to screen it on video or DVD in one of their private screening cabins. Recent *Cinémathèque* retrospectives featured Thai films, the works of Spanish director Pedro Almodovar and America's George Cukor.

51 rue de Bercy, 12th Arr., Métro: Bercy, Tel: 01 71 19 33 33

French School of Seduction *(Ecole Française de Séduction)*... If you are dead serious about learning the fine art of French seduction, you will be pleased to know that there is actually a school that teaches such a course. The *Ecole Française de Séduction* (the French School of Seduction) was founded in 1995 by Véronique J. Corniola, a savvy and polished former marriage counselor with keen insight into this realm of human social interaction. The school functions as sort of a "finishing school for seduction."

The school's instructors begin with the social basics: how to properly carry and present yourself; how to be bold and project self-confidence; the importance of maintaining eye contact; and most important of all, how to nonchalantly strike up a conversation with a promising prospect while shopping for eggplant at the *marché* (market).

The focus is on teaching the students how to discover and to project their very own personal brand of charisma. If all of this sounds a little bit like the plot of the film *Dirty Rotten Scoundrels* (shot in the South of France)—well, the school provides the tools, and how you choose to utilize your newly found skills is up to you.

The program includes extensive hands-on instruction in the field where the instructor stealthily observes while you make attempts to chat-up an unsuspecting subject using the school's techniques. This is followed by a thorough critique and more fieldwork until you achieve the desired level of self-confidence. There is simply no viable alternative to real world experience where practice does indeed make perfect.

But why, you ask, is such a school even necessary in France, supposedly the land of homegrown Don Juans and *femmes fatales?* Well—there are always some out there in the vast gene pool who need a little extra coaching, even in the capital of seduction and romance.

The concept should not be taken lightly. The course of instruction is a very serious endeavor requiring a significant commitment of time and resources. Many former students claim that it has literally changed their lives. Americans and Brits in particular—who many suggest are socially challenged in the realm of flirtation—might benefit from the course.

Branches in Paris and Lyon continue to launch their enlightened students into an unsuspecting world armed with a newfound sense of self-confidence, charm and panache.

55, rue Sainte-Anne, 2nd Arr., Métro: Pyramides, Tel: 01 42 61 84 45, www.ecoledeseduction.com/english/index.html E-mail: ecoledeseduction.veronique@libertysurf.fr

Jim Haynes' Sunday Soirée... Perhaps the best-known American in Paris, Jim Haynes has been hosting Sunday Night Soirées for 28 years. It is said that he has introduced over 100,000 people and is responsible for countless love affairs and dozens of marriages. His Sunday dinner and mixer is held in his Paris *atelier* where about 70 people from all over the world gather to dine, drink and enjoy themselves. The group ranges in age from 25 to 50 and is about one-third French, one-third Anglo and one-third everything else. Telephone Jim Haynes on Sat or Sun for your reservation, directions and the door code. The cost is very reasonable.

Jim Haynes Atelier... 83 rue de la Tombe Issoire, 14th Arr., Metro Alesia, Tel: 01 43 27 17 67, www.jim-haynes.com/contact/index.php, jim_haynes@wanadoo.fr

Casinos in Paris... For those interested in gaming, there are a number of casinos in the Paris region. To assure admission be sure to bring your passport and dress appropriately (no jeans or sneakers).

Aviation Club de France (Casino)... 184 avenue des Champs-Élysées, 8th Arr., Métro: George V, Tel: 01 45 63 32 91, www.avaitionclubdefrance.com

An elegant casino opened in 1907, sporting wood-paneled walls and deep leather chairs. It has more of the feel of a private London social club than a traditional casino. Games available include blackjack, baccarat, poker and backgammon. There are no roulette, slots or dice games. Non-alcoholic drinks are free. A handsome restaurant, bar and lounge are available for dining and socializing. Open 24/7.

Casino Barriére d'Enghein-les-Bains... 3 avenue de Centure, Enghien-les-Bains, Tel: 01 39 34 12 91, www.lucienbarriere.com

This is the largest and most luxurious casino in the Paris region. The resplendent main rooms were built in 1901. Located in an enchanted lakeside setting, the casino complex is 8 miles (14 kilometers) north-east of the central city. Games include blackjack, English roulette, French roulette, stud poker and Punto Banco. A modern annex houses 350 slot machines, two restaurants, bars and a theater.

Friday Night Fever—Paris Roller... Every Friday night (weather permitting) rollerbladers take to the Paris streets in the largest rollerblading event in the world. As many as 10,000 (no, that's not a typo) locals and visitors race along a 17 mile route through the major streets of the capital escorted by a phalanx of French gendarmes in cars and dozens more on rollerblades. The Friday event is limited to experienced rollerbladers. A similar event is held on Sunday for novices and families. Info Fri: www.pari-roller.com or Tel: 01 43 36 89 81

Info Sun: www.rollers-coquillages.org or Tel: 01 44 54 07 44.

Small but very Memorable Museums... Almost everyone is familiar with the large, major museums so alternatively we recommend several of the smaller, more intimate museums where the collections can be viewed in an hour or two. Figuratively speaking, these serve as a refined and satisfying appetizer as opposed to the very filling ten-course meal provided by the Louvre, Musée d'Orsay and others.

Montmartre Museum of Erotic Art *(Musée de l'Erotisme)...* In 1998, erotic art collectors Joseph Khalifa and Alain Plumey opened the *Musée de l'Erotisme* in the Pigalle quarter of Montmartre, not far from the Moulin Rouge. Located in a smart 19th-century townhouse, formerly a cabaret, this well-presented collection of international erotica includes painting, sculpture, graphics, cartoons, artifacts, video and photography.

The museum is thought provoking, humorous and bizarre but never boring. It has been very popular, attracting over 170,000 visitors annually.

72 blvd de Clichy, 18th Arr., Métro: Blanche or Pigalle, Tel: 01 42 58 28 73, www.eroticmuseum.net

Jacquemart André Museum *(Musee Jacquemart André)...* This is one of the finest small museums in the city. This collection was amassed by the nineteenth-century collector Edouard André and his wife Nélie Jacquemart. It includes five thousand works of art, antiquities, frescoes and furnishings primarily from the Italian Renaissance, but also representing the Flemish and French schools of the 17th and 18th centuries. Works by artists such as Rembrandt, Carpaccio, Donatello, Canaletto and Fragonard are on display. The opulent 19th century mansion itself is a wonder to behold and your visit will certainly be memorable. Rental of the audio guide is highly recommended.

58, blvd Haussmann, 8th Arr., Métro: Miromesnil, Tel: 01 45 62 11 59

Rodin Museum *(Musée Rodin)...* Formerly Rodin's luxurious home, the museum displays thousands of his works in terracotta, plaster, bronze, marble, wax, molten glass, and stoneware. Paintings, drawings and works by other artists (Monet, Renoir, Van Gogh) are from his personal collection. The splendid walled sculpture garden is spread over three hectares and contains many of his major works and a small tea room set under the massive linden trees. It is a fine place to spend a sunny afternoon.

77 rue de Varenne, 7th Arr. Métro: Varenne, Tel: 01 44 18 61 10

Museum of the Romantic Life *(Musée de la Vie Romantique)*... The museum is dedicated to the writers, poets and painters of the Romantic Period. This section of Montmartre was the home to numerous artists and intellectuals including Eugene Delacroix, Frédéric Chopin, Georges Sand, Giacomo Rossini and Théodore Géricault. Located in the former home of 19th century romantic painter Ary Sheffer, the museum includes a presentation of Sheffer's *atelier* (studio) in its original state with his original work and others of the period.

The visitor will find the *atelier* filled with golden light bathing the splendid portraits, hung on ocher walls. This quaint Italianate house is tucked away on a charming cobblestone alleyway. The ground floor features the Georges Sand collection with memorabilia including portraits, furnishings, jewelry and letters. The small garden is a relaxing oasis for tea and light refreshments.

16 rue Chaptal, 9th Arr., Métro: St-Georges, Tel: 01 48 74 95 38

The Kitchen Affair... In the late 1990s, my good friend Robert Price, a well-known attorney from San Antonio, was living in a small *pied-a-terre* on rue du Vaugirard, in the 6th Arrondissement. In a spur-of-the-moment decision, Robert's usual interest in art history turned to *haute cuisine.* He enrolled in a course at the internationally famous culinary institute *Le Cordon Bleu,* where Julia Child learned French cooking in the 1950s. While his French was quite serviceable and he would certainly deny it, I have long suspected that he thought he was applying for the "six-day" course and not "six-month" course. Instead of his fellow students being a few New York foodies taking a quick class in preparing French canapés, his cohorts were all highly motivated apprentice chefs, caterers, and budding restaurateurs from Japan, Latin America, Europe and of course, France. To put it simply, it appeared he had bitten off more than he could chew. But to his great credit he stuck it out, putting in grueling 12-hour days learning the French way to cut, blanch, braise, bake and slather heaps of rich Normandy butter onto everything in sight. He created some very tantalizing French dishes during his gastronomic stint. We know because he shared them with his grateful friends.

Naturally Le Cordon Bleu offers less rigorous one and two day courses for those not quite so dedicated. And nothing is quite as appealing as flirting in the kitchen, so consider taking a workshop with your romantic partner. Many a student has met a passionate paramour over a hot stove.

Classes presented by the school's master chefs (often from the best restaurants of Paris) provide an opportunity to create: complex French dishes, soups, chocolates, deserts, foie gras, sauces, and bread (to name only a few choices). These hands-on classes range from a half-day to four days. (Six months for the professional course).

Le Cordon Bleu Paris... 8 rue Léon Delhomme, 15th Arr., Métro: Vaugirard, Tel: 01 53 68 22 50, www.cordonbleu.edu, paris@cordonbleu.edu

Parler-Parlor French-English Conversation Group... Want to practice your French language skills and meet interesting people, all without the bother of having to enroll in a class? Parler-Parlor meets three times a week at several locations around the city. The French-English conversation group is managed by Marie-Elisabeth Crochard (a past director of the Berlitz Language School) and Adrian Leeds. First attendance is free. Call or email for times and locations.

www.parlerparlor.com, Tel: 01 48 42 26 10 or 01 40 27 97 59. info@parlerparlor.com

Classical Concerts at Sainte Chapelle... Magical candle-lit classical & chamber music concerts are held periodically in this awe inspiring chapel built in 1240. La Sainte Chapelle is situated on the *Ile de la Cité,* in the center of Paris, not far from Notre Dame. Purchase tickets at Sainte Chapelle or online at

www.concertics.com, 4 boulevard du Palais, Métro: Cité.

Rendezvous at Parc de Bagatelle... The Park Bagatelle *(Parc de Bagatelle)* is a lovely and highly romantic oasis of ponds laden with water lilies, garden paths and green landscapes. The unusual park within a park (it is within the grounds of the Bois de Boulogne) is enclosed by a high stone wall and it houses a *petit château* built by the Count d'Artois in 1777. He famously bet his sister-in-law Marie Antoinette that it could be constructed in 90 days. He used over 1000 skilled carpenters, artisans and craftsmen to win the bet. There is a small charge (€1.50) to enter Bagatelle. Have a light lunch in a quaint stone pavilion or dine at a table under the shady trees. The splendid little park has long served as a major rendezvous point for Parisians who wish to clandestinely meet their mistress or lover in a discreet out of the way locale.

Parc de Bagatelle, Bois de Boulogne, 16th Arr., Métro: Porte Maillot, Tel: 01 40 67 97 00, Open 9:00 am to dusk.

Place Furstenberg after Dark... For a purely serene and memorable moment, find your way to *place Furstenberg,* said to be the smallest public square in Paris and surely one of the most romantic. Just a very short walk from the bustling center of St-Germain-des-Prés, you can quietly savor the timeless quality of Parisian architecture under the atmospheric glow of the single ornamental street lamp.

Sunday Night Dinner in Paris... Part of the charm of Paris is that it still clings to the tradition of closing most retail, entertainment and restaurant venues on Sunday, a day dedicated to the family. So you will find that many of your favorite restaurants are likely to be closed. The solution is to head for the Marais quarter where shops and restaurants remain open on Sunday. A couple of very appealing restaurants in the Marais:

Chez Omar... 47 rue Bretagne, 3rd Arr., Metro: Filles du Calvaire, Tel: 01 42 72 36 26, Moderate

This friendly bistro is said by many to serve the best traditional Couscous in Paris. The Moroccan dishes come in very generous portions, attracting a large and loyal crowd of fashionista regulars. The good-humored owner, Omar Guerida hovers over the operation, table hopping to keep the clientele well fed and happy. Cuisine: try Omar's *Couscous Royale,* a huge steaming platter of grilled, skewered lamb, spicy *merguez* sausage, chicken and vegetables. They also serve classic bistro fare including a terrific steak & frites with peppercorn sauce. Reasonably priced wine list. Traditional bistro décor; laid back and casual dress. Closed for "lunch" Sunday but open for dinner. One of the author's favorite ethnic restaurants.

La Brasserie Bofinger... 5-7 de la Bastille, 4th Arr., Métro: Bastille, Tel: 02 42 72 87 82, Moderate

Certainly one of the most memorable brasseries in Paris, Bofinger serves fine cuisine in the Alsatian style. A stone's throw from the place Bastille, the Belle Epoque interior is a registered and protected national monument. Dine under a massive stained-glass dome in the main dining room or on black leather banquettes in the smaller, wood paneled salon. Cuisine: home made fois gras, roast leg of lamb, lobster, fresh oysters and their splendid Alsatian *choucroute* (sauerkraut). Try the seafood sauerkraut with monkfish, haddock, salmon and prawns. (Reservations well in advance are necessary for this very popular venue, particularly for the main dining room). If you choose to arrive by taxi, don't tell the driver - Brasserie *BOW finger* (like the fingers used to draw an archer's bow) – he won't have a clue – the pronunciation is *bow fawn jhay.*

For other restaurants located in the Marais, check out the site: www.parismarais.com/selected-restaurants.htm

Erotic Bookstores *(Libraries Érotique)*... The richness of French literature and the titillation of classic erotica will stir the fertile imagination. The following Parisian bookstores (referred to as *libraries* in France) specialize in erotic literature and photography.

Curiosa... 7 rue Crébillon, 6th Arr. Métro: Odéon, Tel: 01 40 46 01 15, www.enfer.com/bookshop.asp

This is one of the city's most substantial erotic bookstores, located near the Luxembourg Gardens, in the fashionable 6th Arr. The offerings range from rare bibliophile treasures and classics of French literature to the art of erotic photography. It is a shop for the collector as well as the connoisseur.

Librarie-Galerie Les Larmes d'Éros... 58, rue Amelot, 11th Arr., (near the Bastille) Métro: Chemin Vert, Tel: 01 43 38 33 43, www.erosconnexion.com

Geared primarily to the collector, this eclectic bookstore and gallery buys and sells ancient and contemporary erotic art and books (earlier than 1950). Their collection includes out-of-print items as well as engravings, photographs and art objects.

La Musardine... 122 rue du Chemin Vert, 11th Arr., Métro: Père Lachaise, Tel: 01 49 29 48 55

This bookstore on the east side of Paris has a collection of over 8,000 books ranging from classic erotic literature to sexy manga and everything in between. They have a notable selection of coffee-table books related to erotic photography.

Librarie de l'Avenue Henri-Veyrier... 31 rue Lecuyer, Saint-Ouen, (on the edge of Paris) Métro: Porte de Clignancourt, Tel: 01 40 11 95 85

An enormous trader of erotica located in the famous Saint-Ouen Flea Market *(Marché aux Puce)* just on the northern edge of the city.

Galleries - Erotica & Collectibles

Au Bonheur du Jour... 11 rue Chabanais, 2nd Arr. Métro: Bourse, Tel: 01 42 96 58 64

This gallery has a splendid collection of 19th and 20th century erotic photographs, books and antique artifacts.

A l'Enseigne des Oudin... 58 rue Quincampoix, 4th Arr. Métro: Les Halles, Tel: 01 42 71 83 65

A well-known gallery featuring edgy work by artists such as Man Ray, Molinier, Lapicque and Maccheroni.

"Good Americans,
when they die,
go to Paris."

~ Oliver Wendell Holmes
(1858) ~

Chapter Ten:
Paris as Therapy

Chapter Ten:

What do Johnny Depp, Edgar Allen Poe, George Plimpton, Carl Jung, Julia Child, Norman Mailer, Harriet Beecher Stowe, James Baldwin, Marc Chagall and Jim Morrison all have in common? The answer is: they were all restless expatriates who at one point in their lives moved to Paris in a quest for inspiration, renewal, or social emancipation. The city has traditionally attracted those who desire to live, work and study in a progressive environment conspicuously instilled with intellectual and artistic freedom. Many were drawn by the city's cultivated tolerance for émigrés and iconoclasts of every stripe, while others simply wanted to escape from the narrow-minded Puritanism back home. Let's be honest, in comparison to the Bohemian excesses of Paris, almost anywhere else seems staid and sedate.

For Americans in particular, there has always been a magical attraction to the French capital. Founding fathers Thomas Jefferson, Ben Franklin and John Adams each served a pleasurable stint here as diplomats. Wealthy families sent their sons and daughters to pursue an education, to absorb the culture and to polish their manners in the refined society.

A later burst of licentiousness brought expatriates such as Henry Miller, Cole Porter, and Theodore Dreiser. Each came in search of an *avant garde* muse, learned to fornicate *à la française,* and aquired habits of drink, and dissipation. The Parisian exploits of such notables as Art Buchwald, Jack Kerouac, and the larger than life Ernest Hemingway have become the stuff of legend. Inspired by captivating literature and steamy memoirs, Americans followed in their footsteps, seeking to capture a bit that magical alchemy.

A Sojourn in Paris... Dreamers worldwide continue to imagine that a sabbatical in this beautiful, old world capital is the cathartic balm that will restore their spirit and reinvigorate their featureless lives. While this fanciful view of Paris may be seen by some as a tired cliché, in the eyes of countless, sanguine travelers and would-be residents, Paris still lives up to its billing. So those, earnest and adventurous souls with enough moxie, will still find the means to wind their way there. The myth endures because the city retains its wondrous capacity to provide pilgrims a springboard for their imagination.

North Americans make up a very large segment of tourists visiting France (about 3.6 million). And according to recent statistics from the U.S. Consulate, there are currently about 60,000 American expats residing in Paris and 170,000 throughout the country.

The American community in Paris is eclectic, cutting across social, economic and generational demographics. Among these are a legion of *bourgeois bohèmes* (a social group the French refer to as *"bobos"*), short for young, affluent, socially progressive, urban gentry. One also finds a significant number of baby boomers; that ubiquitous generation of nomads born between 1946 and 1964, who, instilled with the permissive values of the '60s found themselves perfectly suited to a self-indulgent metropolis with an exuberant lifestyle and few moral taboos.

Most expatriates come in search of a better quality of life. Paris, a compact international city (only 38 square miles) is chock-full of architectural wonders; green parks; splendid restaurants; a world class transportation system and attractive, sophisticated denizens. It features genuine, old fashioned neighborhoods where you will soon be enjoying banter with the local butcher, baker and café waiter.

Should one be concerned about the attitude of the French toward Americans? Ask virtually any American who has lived in Paris and they will tell you that it is simply not an issue. Anyway, with the election President Nicolas Sarkozy, it appears that Americans and the French have decided to kiss and make up.

The British also have a love affair with France, (though not necessarily the French). A large number of Brits reside in Paris however they seem to have emigrated in ever larger numbers to the sunny climes of Dordogne, Provence and Languedoc-Roussillon in the South. The number of UK citizen living in France is around 400,000. Acquiring traditional cottages, villas, and farmhouses, they have heartily embraced the "Slow Movement," a lifestyle dedicated to the historical, artistic and environmental heritage of the traditional countryside (particularly the gastronomic pleasures). In the South of France, the two hour lunch not only survives, it is practically mandatory.

Of course, it is never straightforward and painless. Any international relocation, even a temporary one, presents obstacles to be overcome. Those peculiar challenges are not covered in this guide since there are so many excellent books on the subject.

For many the "sabbatical in Paris" is still a hallowed tradition and it may be as simple as exchanging apartments with a current resident who is seeking his or her own sojourn abroad.

The city can be alluring in the extreme; some come for a brief visit and seriously smitten, stay for a lifetime.

***Art de Vivre* (The Art of Living)...** What may Americans and Anglos learn from the French? The art of living; a whole new way of seeing the world around you, based on social rituals and traditions; with less focus on career; more on the rewards of leisure and time well spent with family and friends. Theirs is a 2,000 year old Mediterranean culture, at the center of a cultivated European civilization and they appear to have learned a few lessons along the way.

Chapter Eleven:
Erotic Clubbing

11

Chapter Eleven:

"Of all the sexual aberrations, chastity is the strangest."

~ Anatole France ~

There is an enduring liberal-mindedness among the French concerning all matters related to their personal pursuit of pleasure. Forged by the eighteenth century revolution, *Liberté, Egalité,* and *Fraternité* endowed the individual with the privilege to engage in certain actions without the interference of others. One's personal peccadilloes are seen as utterly private and sacrosanct, giving free reign to define individual moral traits, virtues and vices. They fiercely resist any infringement by the state, organized religion or society upon their intimate affairs.

In this unfettered environment, extraordinary freedom, eccentricity and sexual experimentation flourished in Paris. One of many interludes of self-indulgence appeared at the end of the nineteenth century, an era later christened *La Belle Époque* (the beautiful period). A time of great prosperity fostered the Bohemian culture of Montmartre where a clique of dissident painters, sculptors, and writers shunned the bourgeois society of their parents and descended into eroticism and decadence. The poster boy of the *Belle Époque* was the randy, 4 foot 11 inch Toulouse-Lautrec who, steeped in hallucinogenic absinthe, haunted the neighborhood bars, brothels and cabarets, particularly the Moulin Rouge.

Another memorable period came between the wars (the 20's and 30's) when there was a sharp rise in sexual promiscuity and a breakdown of social taboos. International artists and intellectuals were drawn to Paris including James Joyce, Man Ray, John Dos Passos, and Pablo Picasso.

This giddy sense of sexual freedom reemerged yet again during the unrestrained "free-love" days of the 60's and 70's. A Parisian tolerance of hedonism was ushered in that has never really abated.

Paris Libertine Clubs... Today Parisians often indulge their fantasies behind a non-descript door marked *Club Privé.*

The city is home to over forty private *Clubs Libertins.* These venues are part nightclub, part theme restaurant and part sybaritic rendezvous. Within these cozy social clubs, heterosexual couples as well as male and female singles socialize, flirt, dine, dance and seduce, all on the premises. This is "erotic clubbing" Parisian style. At first glance, they appear to be just like any other bar/lounge/disco, however in addition to the usual amenities, they offer a variety of hidden alcoves, niches and chambers uniquely adapted to facilitate sexual liaisons (either private or shared).

The term libertine, in French *libertin,* comes from the Latin *libertinus* which originally referred to those philosophers who freed themselves from the dogmas and practices of the church. It evolved over time to mean a free-thinker, a person sexually unrestrained by prevailing social convention. This perfectly describes the aficionado of the erotic clubs.

Appealing to the adventurous pleasure seeker, these clubs have become quite popular among all Europeans (but none more so than the French). Since first appearing in the early 1970's the *Clubs Libertins* have become a permanent fixture in the progressive Parisian social milieu.

The Private Club *(Club Privé)*... The *Clubs Libertins* are all "private"; consequently the proprietors retain the right to refuse entrance to anyone they feel does not fit into the "spirit of the club." They are free to establish any entrance criteria they wish, no matter how arbitrary. Club managers suggest that failure to be admitted is most often due to dress code or intoxication issues (about which the clubs are very strict). Just like all of the main-stream dance clubs and discos, decisions are clearly based on personal appearance.

The libertin clubs *(also known as clubs échangistes, clubs de rencontres or boîtes échangistes)* are found in every neighborhood in Paris, including many of the most affluent. An unusually subdued and discreet exterior is typical of these venues, with hardly more than a small brass plaque to identify the location. Almost all clubs require reservations.

Who attends the Clubs?... In the past, erotic clubbing was an amusement indulged in mostly by middle-aged couples whose relationship had run out of sexual energy and excitement, but during the past decade it has become more of a "mainstream" leisure activity in France. The average age of club patrons is still late thirties and early forties, but the phenomenon has also become *branche* (trendy) among fashionable young Parisians in their twenties and early thirties.

The more exclusive venues are ultra selective in their admission policies, favoring a physically attractive crowd that includes many well-to-do professionals. The second tier of clubs are slightly more accessible but still selective.

Clubs like the Overside and Acanthus Paris are not unlike a large traditional discothèque inasmuch as they attract a younger crowd often focused on music and dancing. But the unique aspect of erotic clubbing is that patrons may dispense with a step in the usual process of seduction. Instead of going home for love-making, they may proceed to one of the intimate chambers available within the club.

A visit to a club libertine may be suitable "entertainment" for those couples and singles who in total anonymity seek to break free of customary social conventions, while indulging their various fantasies.

I Like to Watch... Many couples attend simply to immerse themselves in the erotically charged atmosphere but never actually participate with others. This symbiotic relationship between the voyeur and exhibitionist, a kind of *théâtre sensual,* is said to be a principal element in the popularity of the clubs. Regulars suggest that it is an expedient means of stimulating their everyday sex life. "It's become a leisure activity, like going to the theatre or the cinema," said Alain Plumey, curator of the Musée de l'Erotisme in Paris.

How an Evening Progresses... You arrive at the club, ring the buzzer and the host greets you at the door. This is the point at which you will be closely screened. The entry fee usually entitles you one or more complimentary drinks. The better Parisian clubs have a restaurant on the premises so many patrons begin the evening with dinner. Alternativly most venues provide a complimentary buffet for guests. After dinner, patrons gather in the bar/lounge or on the dance floor. As one might imagine in this uninhibited atmosphere, the dancing becomes pretty erotic.

Patrons eventually gravitate to the pool, sauna or Jacuzzi and from there to the *salons intimes* (intimate chambers). These areas are comfortably furnished boudoirs of varying sizes with large, overstuffed sofas, beds, massage tables and other appropriate furnishings. Some clubs encourage sexual playfulness with a "dark room," a blacked-out chamber where one may explore his/her fellow patrons in total anonymity. Spacious shower facilities (amply supplied with the necessary toiletries) are provided allowing attendees to freshen up.

Club Entrance Policies & Etiquette... Many clubs are restricted exclusively to couples, while others admit both couples and some singles *(mixte).* If clubs admit female and/or male singles, they often do so only during limited hours (usually in the afternoon or early evening).

The screeners at the door are strict because managers are highly focused on creating a comfortable, relaxed atmosphere. They welcome well-dressed, well-behaved guests but will rapidly eject anyone who does not rigidly adhere to the club's code of behavior. It is a standard rule that persons who arrive together must leave together, permitting the club to maintain an appropriate gender balance.

Under French law one must be at least 18 years of age to enter. Condoms are mandatory, and patrons will insist on their use (they are distributed free at the bar). The term for condom is *preservatif.* All of the clubs referred to in this chapter are "exclusively" heterosexual. However, bisexuality among female patrons is relatively common.

Paris has an active gay and lesbian community with a wide selection of gay and lesbian clubs. See Chapter 12 on Gay & Lesbian Paris.

Dress Code... You will very likely be turned away at the door if you are not wearing appropriate attire. Most female patrons wear overtly provocative attire. And of course, don't forget the all-important high heels.

It may "sexist" by Anglo-American standards, but women will rarely be admitted to a club wearing slacks. Men should wear a jacket or at least stylish trousers and a dress shirt. In the top tier clubs, dress is elegant, so jacket and tie may be mandatory. Women should select their best matching lingerie because within the club, this is what they may be wearing to lounge about. When in doubt regarding the dress code, inquire when making reservations.

Single Men *(Hommes Seuls)* & Single Women *(Femmes Seules)*... For reasons that are obvious, managers make a concerted effort to maintain a gender balance. In addition to afternoon singles hours, some clubs admit a very limited number of single men and women during evening couple's hours. But like nightclubs of every type, libertine clubs uphold a severe double standard favoring single women.

Special Theme Evenings *(Soirées a Theme)*... To add variety to the menu, most clubs advertise special "theme evenings." For instance, they may promote a special evening for Valentine's Day *(Soirée Saint-Valentin),* Asian Night

(Soirée Asiatique), Pajama Party *(Soirée Pyjama)* or Mixed Couples & Singles Evening *(Soirée Mixte).*

List of Libertine Clubs *(Clubs Libertins):*

Les Chandelles... 1 rue Thérese, 1st Arr. (Located near the Opéra) Métro: Pyramides, Tel: 01 42 60 43 31, www.les-chandelles.com, E-mail: club@les-chandelles.com

Amenities: Stylish club, restaurant, bar/lounge, dance floor, showers

Hours: Tues–Sat evening open 10:30 pm to dawn

Mon - Fri afternoons open 4:00 to 10:00 pm; Restaurant: Mon–Sat 9:30 pm

Entry fee: Afternoons – couples €15, singles €39; Evenings – Couples €76, no singles

Many upscale Parisians make this club their sensual playground and it has a reputation for enforcing the most severe door policy and dress code of all the clubs. Patrons tend to be attractive, sexy and relatively youthful (20s to early 40s). The clientele ranges from professional athletes to stars to government ministers. On weeknights one might see 25 couples in attendance and on Saturday as many as 70 couples. When full, the spacious club is a sexual frolic from one end to the other. The intimate spaces have been cleverly designed to facilitate one's voyeuristic inclinations. The dedicated staff provide first class service, maintaining the entire facility as one would a luxury hotel.

Acanthus Paris... 607 avenue du Lys 77190 Dammarie lès Lys, Tel: 01 60 63 73 09, www.clubacanthus.com, info@acanthus.be

Hours: Fri, Sat & Sun- 8:00 pm to 5:00 am

Entry fee: Fri & Sun - couples €60, single men permitted €80, single women €30, dinner incl. 3 drinks

Sat - couples €60 incl. 3 drinks, €90 for dinner incl. 3 drinks, single women €30 incl. 3 drinks or €45 for dinner incl 3 drinks

Set in a sumptuous chateau, this exotic club is situated in a small village about 31 miles (49 kilometers) from Paris. This new concept in libertinage has been an enormous success since opening in October of 2005, providing patrons with an environment of relaxation and elegance. The bold, contemporary interior contrasts with, and complements the building's 18th century exterior. Luxurious amenities include a world-class discotheque and sound system, fine restaurant, two bars, intimate chambers and a spacious sauna/hammam. A fashionable and attractive crowd is assured by the highly selective door policy and dress code (it simply states "visitors should be dressed in an elegant and sexy way)."

Saturday is the biggest party night (couples only) with large crowds, while Friday evenings are designed to accommodate singles. In order to maintain the appropriate ratio, one single is admitted for each couple admitted. Special theme evenings are announced in advance on the Acanthus website or via email. The availability of lockers to store clothes and personal belongings is a nice touch. Overnight accommodations may be found at nearby hotels should you decide to stay over.

Overside... 92 rue du Cherche Midi, 6th Arr., Métro: Vaneau, Tel: 01 42 84 10 20, Open to couples & singles, www.overside.fr/english/presentation/start.htm

Hours: Wed to Sun, couples only 10:30 pm to dawn (Wed & Sun evenings open to singles)

Amenities: bar, large dance floor, lounge, 7 salons intimes decorated in various themes and a quality buffet.

Entry fee: couples €67, including one drink each, singles €108

Consistently a top choice in erotic clubbing among the younger, stylish set (age 25 to 40). Club habitués come to dance and romp in a wild and free-spirited fashion not possible in a regular discotheque. The large dance floor, talented DJ, great music selection and cozy boudoirs attract a loyal following of beautiful people. Overside is conveniently located in the heart of St-Germain-des-Prés, near the Bon Marche department store. Good staff attitude, convivial management and an atmosphere highly charged with erotic energy.

No Comment Club... 36 rue de Ponthieu, 8th Arr., (near Champs Élysées), Métro: St-Philippe-du-Roule, Tel: 01 43 59 23 95, Couples only, www.nocommentclub.com

Hours: Tues–Sat: from 11:00 pm

Restaurant—Thurs, Fri, Sat: from 9:30 pm

Amenities: Restaurant, 2 bars, dance floor, buffet

Entry fee: couples €68, includes 1 drink

Warmly furnished, the No Comment Club features fine antiques, wood panelling, and beamed ceilings. The designers have paid considerable attention to detail in the salons, restaurant and playrooms, where the highly seductive ambiance is enhanced with mood lighting. One boudoir features a four poster bed the size of your average living room. Two handsome and clubby bars, complimentary buffet and a pleasant staff.

Chris & Manu... 5 rue Saint-Bon, 4th Arr., Métro: Hôtel de Ville, Tel: 01 42 72 52 18, Open to couples only, http://c4.lxir.net/www/chris-manu/en/Default.php

Hours: Tues–Sat 10:30 pm to sunrise.

Restaurant: Tues–Sat 8:30 pm.

Amenities: Restaurant, bar/lounge, dance floor, showers

Entry fee: Couples €60, includes 2 drinks

Chris & Manu is a very well established top-tier Parisian club, having been founded in 1983. Good dance floor and intriguing *salons intime.* Located in the 4th Arrondissement near City Hall *(Hotel de Ville),* the club is spread over three floors (with more than 450 square meters) and attracts a BCBG crowd. The club owes part of its notoriety to famed French author and intellectual Michel Houellebecq, who described a scene at Chris & Manu in his best-selling novel *Les Particules Élémentaires.* Selective door policy, attractive crowd, and cordial staff/management.

Le Nautilus... 18 rue Feydeau, 2nd Arr., Métro: Bourse, Tel: 01 40 41 98 58, Open to couples only, www.lenautilus.net

Hours: Afternoons Mon to Fri 1:00 to 8:00 pm; evenings Wed to Sat from 10:30pm.

Entry fee: Couples €49 afternoon, €65 evening including one drink

The theme of Le Nautilus is a Jules Verne submarine with lots of bulkheads and portholes throughout. There are secluded alcoves decorated with comfortable settees in this small, well-maintained club. In case you have ever had an overwhelming urge to play roulette in the nude, they schedule various theme nights including a "Las Vegas-style Casino Night"

Le Club 2+2... 9 Boulevard Edgar Quinet, 14th Arr., Métro: Edgar Quinet, Tel: 01 43 35 14 00, Open to couples only, www.2plus2.fr

Hours: 7 days a week, 2:00 pm to sunrise.

Restaurant: Menu 30€; open 8:00 pm to midnight

Amenities: Restaurant, bar/lounge, dance floor

Entry fee: €33 per couple evenings, €26 afternoon

Dress code: Dresses or skirts for women, no trousers; men smart attire.

In operation for 27 years, Le Club 2 + 2 is another of the more famous libertine clubs in Paris and one that appeals to an over 40 clientele. The red and gold décor is reminiscent of old Paris. Restaurant offers a prix fixe menu at €34.

Quai 17... 15-17 quai de l'Oise, 19th Arr., Métro: Crimee, Tel: 01 42 05 64 64, Couples and singles at all hours.

Hours: Tues - Fri from 9:00 pm, Sat from 10:00 pm, Sun from 9:00 pm. Bistro, opens at 9:30 pm

Entry fees: Couples €50, Women €15, Men €100

Amenities: Bar, bistro, dance floor, www.quai17.net/index.php

Located in the Villette quarter of the 19th Arrondissment, Quai 17 is frequented by more singles than most clubs. The 500 square meter club has a lively disco organized around a central bar.

Au Plurial Club... 13 rue Francois Miron, 4th Arr., Métro: Hotel de Ville, Tel: 01 40 29 07 52, www.plurielclub.com/index_us.htm, Couples and singles at all hours.

Amenities: Bar, comfortable rooms, buffet, free condoms.

Hours: Opens Tues – Sat at 8:00 pm, buffet every evening, closed Sun & Mon

Entry fees: Couples €58, Women €24, Men €98, including 1 drink plus buffet

This club is located in an historic 14th century building in the Marais, a stone's throw from Paris City Hall. It features four floors of playrooms and also caters to singles.

“Of all possible sexual perversions, religion is the only one to have ever been scientifically systematized.”

~ Louis Aragon ~

Erotic Entertainment

The "New Civilized" Strip Tease Clubs... It never ceases to amaze how concepts go in and out of fashion in Paris. Strip tease has recently returned in an entirely new, polished mode. And in the interest of gender equality most venues now also feature entertainment for the ladies.

Stringfellow's Cabaret of Angels... 27 avenue des Ternes, 17th Arr., Métro: Ternes, Tel: 01 47 66 45 00

Opened by British nightclub impresario Peter Stringfellow, this chic club, catering to a cosmopolitan crowd, provides a stimulating combination of strip tease and lap dancing. Patrons may choose from about forty dancers, with male dancers available for the ladies.

Pink Paradise... 49-51 rue de Ponthieu, 8th Arr. Métro: Franklin D. Roosevelt, Tel: 01 58 36 19 20

Owners Cathy and David Guetta have created an American-style striptease establishment with tasteful décor, subdued lighting and drop-dead gorgeous dancers. Or, you may opt for a private dancer in your own secluded alcove. One Sunday per month, the club schedules a special theme night soiree exclusively for the ladies (Girls and the City) featuring hot male strippers.

Strip just for the Ladies

Le Wagg (Club)... 62 rue Mazarine, 6th Arr., Métro: Odéon, Tel: 06 74 62 00 83, www.dlpevenements.com/lolita

Every Thursday from 7:00 to 9:00 pm, Le Wagg hosts a special ladies night billed as the *"LoLiTa HappyHour."* Open to ladies only but males are admitted after 9:00 pm when the female crowd has been sufficiently "warmed up." Thoughtful amenities include massages and manicures for the patrons.

Regines... 49/51 rue de Ponthieu, 8th Arr., Métro: Franklin Roosevelt, Tel: 01 43 59 21 13, http://www.bonheur-des-dames.com/accueil.html

Regines presents *Au Bonheur des Dames,* a feminine spectacular on Thursdays from 9:30 to 11:00 pm. Ladies only – admission free; males permitted after 11:30pm.

"It is not enough
to conquer;
one must know
how to seduce."

~ *Voltaire* ~

Chapter Twelve:
Gay & Lesbian Paris

12

Chapter Twelve:

The center of Parisian gay nightlife is the Marais district with its lively mix of bars, clubs, cafés and restaurants, intermingled with straight bars and fashionable shops, all accentuated by the quarter's cobblestone streets and ancient architecture. Les Halles district is also home to a number of popular gay venues.

Bars & Cafés

Amnesia Café... 42 rue Vieille du Temple, 4th Arr., Métro: St-Paul, Tel: 01 42 72 16 94

This relaxed lounge bar with a friendly atmosphere attracts a young professional crowd. Large banquettes, leather armchairs, a comfortable dining area and the cheerful happy hour give it the right stuff. Music: disco, pop, R&B.

Banana Café... 13 rue de la Ferronnerie, 1st Arr., Métro: Châtelet, Tel: 01 42 72 16 94

A crowded all-night venue with over the top décor, go-go dancers and a popular "sing-along" around the basement piano. Theme nights attract delightfully outrageous costumes. Music: techno & house.

La Champmeslé... 4 rue Chabanais, 2nd Arr., Métro: Pyramides, Tel: 01 42 96 85 20

This legendary lesbian bar first opened way back in 1979. The 300-year-old stone walls and ceiling beams add ambiance to a convivial saloon where a mixed international crowd gathers on Thurs and Sat evenings for cabaret.

Le Tropic Café... 66 rue des Lombards, 1st Arr., Métro: Châtelet, Tel: 01 40 13 92 62

A lively café-bar in the heart of the Les Halles district with a young and appealing clientele. Great kitsch décor and free flowing drinks.

Open Café... 17 rue des Archives, 4th Arr., Métro: Hôtel de Ville, Tel: 01 42 72 26 18

Virtually a gay institution in the heart of the Marais, the Open Café is a must for locals and visitors alike. The small terrace is prime "see and be seen" territory. Check out the genderless restrooms *(les WC).*

Le Raidd... 23 rue du Temple, 4th Arr., Métro: Hôtel de Ville Tel: 01 42 77 04 88

A highly rated bar/club in the Marais featuring fabulous music, muscled barmen and exceptional DJs. Le Raidd is particularly well-known for its boisterous "Shower Show" that runs four times nightly. The bar stays open until 4:00 am.

Le Pulp... 25 bd. Poissonnière, 2nd Arr., Métro: Grands Boulevards, Tel: 01 40 26 01 93

Le Pulp is by far the trendiest lesbian disco in the city, packed wall to wall with celebrants. The dance club has a strict door policy, so long lines are common. The seriously burgundy décor is reminiscent of a 19th century French music hall. Friendly staff. Music: disco, techno.

Le Depot... 10 rue aux Ours, 3rd Arr., Métro: Étienne Marcel, Tel: 01 44 54 96 96

Located near the Centre Pompidou, Le Depot is probably the largest and certainly the most famous cruise club in France, with a massive dance floor, a labyrinth of private backrooms and a gigantic darkroom in the *sous sol* (basement). Sat and Sun evenings are rousing and tumultuous until sunrise. The Sun afternoon tea dance (starting at 5:00 pm) is very well-attended.

“Never lose sight of
the fact that all
human felicity lies
in man’s imagination,
and that he cannot think
to attain it unless
he heeds all his caprices.
The most fortunate
of persons is he
who has the most means
to satisfy his vagaries.”

~ *Marquis de Sade*
(1740–1814) ~

Chapter Thirteen:

Dangerous Liaisons–Fantasy, Fetish & Fashion

Missing Your Moment in History... Ah! How frivolous and fickle history can be in anointing its heroes and villains.

On the 4th of July 1789, the infamous author, philosopher and unrepentant raconteur, Donatien Alphonse François Marquis de Sade was transferred from the dungeon of the Bastille in Paris, where he was serving a long prison sentence, to the lunatic asylum in nearby Charenton. The reason for his transfer, no doubt due to some obscure bureaucratic decision, is now long forgotten. De Sade had been imprisoned at "His Majesty's Pleasure," which is to say, by virtue of a *lettre de cachet* (a decree signed by the King) because he espoused extreme freedom in the pursuit of personal pleasure and repeatedly dallied with servants, nuns and prostitutes, to the great dismay of his long-suffering wife. In addition, he broadly indulged his taste for anti-clerical blasphemy and bizarre sexual theatricality. De Sade was considered "scandalous" by the standards of his era and his family had successfully sought to have him removed from society.

Only ten days after his transfer an angry Parisian mob stormed the Bastille freeing from imprisonment fewer than ten small-time miscreants and common criminals, but setting in motion one of the most momentous events in world history—the French Revolution.

So by a mere fluke of timing the Marquis was not present in the Bastille on that eventful day when the rioting masses freed the prisoners from the clutches of their King. Had the Marquis remained in the Bastille, his glorious "liberation" on the 14th of July 1789 would have made him the highest-ranking and the most prominent prisoner freed. Needless to say, French history may have taken a different turn had the notorious Marquis de Sade emerged as the gallant, larger than life hero and champion of the Revolution. The later "Reign of Terror" might have had a decidely more kinky edge.

But alas, the Marquis missed his fateful rendezvous with history and today is remembered as the prolific author of a dozen passionately written novels illuminating his hedonistic philosophy, and explicitly cataloguing his aberrant behavior. And of course, he has been immortalized by lending his name to that particular facet of human eroticism known as "Sadism."

Consistent with the spirit of the Marquis, the city cultivates a variety of exotic venues faithfully celebrating his sexual eccentricities. These unconventional bars and clubs cater to the needs and tastes of French fetishist and BDSM enthusiasts. They are known simply as *Les Clubs Fétichistes.*

Bars & Clubs for Fetishists

Cris et Chuchotements (Cries & Whispers)... 9 rue Truffaut, 17th Arr., Métro: Rome, Tel: 01 42 93 70 21, www.cris-et-chuchotements.com

Hours: Tues to Sat from 10:30 pm–dawn.

Entry fee: couples 40€, includes drink; single males 90€, includes drink

Cris et Chuchotements is the only fully "dedicated" fetish and BDSM club in Paris. It was founded by Pascal, former owner of the infamous Bar-Bar (sadly closed). Handsomely decorated in "high dungeon" style, the club is generously equipped with all of the necessary implements, including chains, handcuffs, masks and other cruel "tools of the trade." The dress code is strictly enforced, so don't even think of showing up in everyday street clothes or you may have to be *severely* punished. There is a wide selection of theme nights accommodating every area of interest. In particular, do not miss the monthly "slave market." Make reservations.

Caves le Chapelais... 7 rue Lechapelais, 17th Arr., Métro: La Fourche, Tel: 01 42 93 76 49

Cave le Chapelais is the venue that hosts the famous *Nuit Élastique,* the largest recurrent fetish party in Paris. Held the second Saturday of the month, *Nuit Élastique* is an extraordinary event for lovers of latex, vinyl and leather. It attracts an eclectic crowd of 300 to 400 who rock the night away to electro, techno and new wave. Do not expect to be admitted unless appropriately attired as a nurse, doctor, uniformed soldier, leather clad dominatrix, tattooed goth, pierced punk or some *outré* version of "Sideshow Bob." *Nuit Élastique* has been a singularly successful Parisian phenomenon for more than eight years.

Sex is as important as eating or drinking and we ought to allow the one appetite to be satisfied with as little restraint or false modesty as the other.

~ *Marquis De Sade (1740–1814)* ~

Fetish Culture & Eroticism from Fashion to Hollywood... In an unambiguous trend widely acknowledged by fashion critics and sociologists alike, fetish style continues to exert an influence on the rarified world of *haute couture.* This look has been evident in the very edgy work of French fashion designers Thierry Mugler and Jean-Paul Gaultier who frequently incorporate fetish and SM imagery into their fashion lines. The late Gianni Versace was known for dressing rock and film stars in his lace-and-leather style known as "hooker chic." Dior's designer John Galliano explored sexual fantasy in his work with high-heeled French maids, slinky models bound in jeweled manacles and in homage to director Federico Fellini, a tightly corseted Catholic bishop. So it came as no surprise when *Vogue* magazine (UK) recently appeared featuring models sporting slick, black latex/PVC leggings, mirroring the vinyl fetish crowd.

In the world of film, historians have long suggested that both the Batman and Catwoman characters are Hollywood's overt representation of fetish culture. And who could forget sex icon Madonna's celebrated stunt, flashing her pointy, bullet-coned corset (naturally designed by Gaultier) to the crowd at the Cannes Film Festival? The event was credited with creating the fashion craze of undergarment as outerwear.

If you found the masked "orgy scene" in Stanley Kubrick's psycho-sexual drama *Eyes Wide Shut* (1999) to be titillating, rest assured that you are not alone. Apparently a significant percentage of the population finds the idea of dressing up in masks, capes and period costumes to be highly stimulating and sexually provocative, as evidenced by the long tradition of erotic Mardi Gras celebrations around the globe. In the ritualized orgy sequence, Kubrick used edgy Romanian incantations played backwards to establish a menacing mood of desire and violence. While the film was controversial, it deftly explored the boundaries between fantasy and reality while attempting to define the dissimilar perceptions men and women have of infidelity.

Mainstream films such as David Lynch's dark and brooding *Mulholland Drive* (2001) pushed the bounds of licentiousness with its auto-erotic, lesbian fantasies and fabulously offbeat characters including a manipulative dwarf and a menacing but philosophical cowboy. For Lynch fans, this was more of the quirky eroticism he served up in *Blue Velvet* and the popular TV series *Twin Peaks.*

In a deliciously kinky screen relationship (*Secretary,* 2002) the obsessive secretary played by Maggie Gyllenhaal fulfills her innermost masochistic longings when she is heartily spanked by her lawyer-boss, played by James Spader. The spanking scene was voted the "Sexiest Moment in Film" according to a survey conducted by Europe's leading online DVD rental company LOVEFiLM.

Certainly not to be outdone in the realm of eroticism, the French have produced innumerable *auteur* films exploring every nuance of extreme sexuality. Catherine Breillat is a controversial, taboo-breaking French director and outspoken feminist, who boldly incorporates the politics of gender into her films. One of Breillat's most provocative techniques is to portray her characters carrying on lengthy, erudite philosophical discussions while engaged in very explicit sex. Her 2004 film *Anatomy of Hell* was a dark mood piece that forced viewers to examine their own assumptions about male – female relations. The film dealt bluntly with issues of dominance, voyeurism and misogyny, and unquestionably broke new ground in the use of "gardening implements".

These examples demonstrate how the fetishism and SM have, not so subtley influenced western popular culture through fashion and cinema. Perhaps the phenomenon is a bit more pronounced in France since the pleasure-obsessed French are unabashedly *avant-garde* about all things *érotique* and are typically far ahead of the curve.

The current trend has seen the adoption of the lifestyle (particularly on the fetish side) by those in "mainstream" society. Many *au currant* young people in their 20's and 30's view fetishism simply as edgy role playing. Certainly there are still many serious and very dedicated aficionados, but it has become more difficult to draw the line between these and the weekend party crowd. So, many ordinary Parisians pull on their leather or vinyl outfits, and head for the local disco for an all night bash where they and their peers enjoy a delicious "anti-social thrill."

Fetish Shopping

Dèmonia... 10 Cité Joly, 11th Arr., Métro: Père Lachaise, Tel: 01 43 14 82 70, www.demonia.com

Hours: Mon–Sat 10:00 am–7:30 pm

Dèmonia is reputed to be the most popular fetish/BDSM boutique in Paris. It is a virtual "Wal-Mart" of accessories and implements, including but not limited to: muzzles, gags, paddles, masks, whips, leashes, leads, floggers, chains, harnesses, shackles, canes, hoods, slings, swings, collars, clamps, corsets, leather, vinyl, latex and lace. And naturally, they carry those snappy *faux* German Army uniforms plus a wide range of other exotic apparel.

Phylea... 61 rue Quincampoix, 4th Arr., Métro: Les Halles, Tel: 01 42 76 01 80

Since 1989, a fetish fashion boutique dedicated to seduction with imagination, offering stylish ready-to-wear and made-to-order costumes. They carry corsets, leather, latex, vinyl and fine silk lingerie.

Theatrhall... 3 carrefour de l'Odéon, 6th Arr., Métro: Odéon, Tel: 01 43 26 64 90, www.theatrhall.com

Perhaps you plan to attend a costume party, or a period masked ball, or you simply like dressing up in an 18th century style waistcoat, lace shirt, cape, hat, wig and mask for a naughty *"Eyes Wide Shut"* frolic with your favorite companion. In either case, you will be hard-pressed to find a better period *costumier* than Theatrhall.

La Nuit Dèmonia... A tall, lean, attractive woman with her long blond hair gathered back into an understated ponytail, strides resolutely down the sidewalk of the boulevard de Clichy. The woman has that haughty, bored, French bourgeois look so often seen in film on the face of actress Catherine Deneuve. The milling crowd of tourists, tightly gathered for the evening performance at Le Moulin Rouge, parts quickly to make way while staring in flustered awe. She is wearing a finely tailored, skin-tight, black leather outfit with a handsome, equestrienne-style, silk top hat. The onlookers gawk as they observe that in heightened contrast to her shiny, black attire, she has long, white, feathered angel wings extending down her back, almost to the knees. The heels of her thigh-high, black, leather boots click loudly on the concrete as this kinky, angelic vision leads a stooped, slightly built man by a long chain attached to his studded leather collar. Her slave obediently follows as she disappears into the entrance of the Locomotive Disco.

Welcome to *La Nuit Dèmonia!* The famous Demonia boutique annually sponsors an enormous, not-to-be-missed event, known far and wide to loyal members of the European fetish community. *La Nuit Demonia* features an all-night disco dance, fashion show and gala procession, all festively held at the celebrated Locomotive Disco, located next door to the Moulin Rouge.

To adhere to the strict dress code for this grand *soirée* one should arrive attired in the uniform of a pilot, maidservant, soldier, doctor, nurse or police officer. Uniforms and garments made from leather, vinyl, or latex are naturally preferred. Other eccentric attire such as that worn by our angel is permitted as well. The spectacle is a major draw for European bondage *maîtresses* and masters as well as their submissive acolytes. It is said that enthusiastic devotees travel from as far as South America, Canada, the US, UK, Germany, Italy, Belgium, Netherlands and Spain to attend this preeminent event on the fetishist calendar. *Nuit Dèmonia* is proudly sponsored in association with *Nuit Élastique* and the Belgian Fetish Assembly. One must be at least 18 years of age to attend. www.nuitdemonia.com

Fetish in Paris... *Fetish in Paris* is considered to be, er, "more mainstream" than the annual *Nuit Demonia* event. It is patronized by a much younger, more in-vogue crowd. Focused primarily on dressing up in fetish character, the attendees at this disco "theme party" come out in latex, leather and vinyl, while dancing to electro, techno, indie, new wave and 80's. The large *Fetish in Paris* events do not attract the hard-core BDSM aficionados. This appears to be a "youth trend" (not unlike grunge, punk, hip-hop) more than the genuine embrace of an alternative life style. One must be at least 18 years of age to attend. See website for schedule - www.fetishinparis.com.

Chapter Fourteen:
Venal Pleasures

“Paris represented the aristocracy of vice, magnificent and untamed.”

~ *Émile Zola, Nana (1891)* ~

“A place for everything, everything in its place.”

~ *Benjamin Franklin, while standing outside of a Paris bordello (1778)* ~

Chapter Fourteen:

During the middle Ages, prostitution was prevalent in every French town regardless of size and often the local government designated areas where the trade was tolerated. In most larger cities, the government established their own municipally operated brothels. The medieval French had a pragmatic view of the trade in that they believed it was immoral, but also felt it was necessary, and prostitutes would be safer in brothels than on the streets.

The Age of the Courtesan... The courtesans of the 16th and 17th centuries were skilled, socially adept professional mistresses who were associated with noblemen and other men of wealth. A classic example of the successful courtesan was Ninon de l'Enclos, one of the most beautiful and flamboyant women of 17th century France. In an era when females were accorded few opportunities to flourish outside of marriage, she rose to the very top of French society, chose her own friends and lovers, amassed a great fortune and maintained a legendary salon. By any measure, she should be viewed as an example of early feminism justified by the freedom she demanded and enjoyed.

Mademoiselle de l'Enclos, who never married, was an intellectual, writer and philosopher of the "Epicurean" movement. She passionately believed that life was intended for the rampant pursuit of pleasure and avoidance of pain. She expounded her philosophy in the novel *The Flirt Avenged* (1659). Numerous men fell under her seductive spell, including La Rochefoucauld, Molière and even the all powerful Cardinal Richelieu. For her, seduction was a grand game employing consummate skills learned over a lifetime. The Duc de Saint-Simon described her as "A shining example of the triumph of vice, when directed with intelligence and redeemed by a little virtue."

Eighteenth Century Bacchanalia... In 1784, Philippe Duc d'Orleans, brother of Louis XV, converted the Palais-Royal into the world's first luxury "shopping mall." The colonnades of the Palais-Royal were bursting with fashionable boutiques, restaurants, gambling houses and upscale brothels. A gathering place for aristocrats, writers and intellectuals, the untamed bacchanalia attracted such historical personalities as Giacomo Casanova and the young Napoleon Bonaparte. Historians suggest that the revolution of 1789 was hatched among its cafés.

Throughout the period of the American Revolutionary War, Benjamin Franklin, the brilliant American ambassador (1778–1785) worked diligently to establish "close relations" with the French. Despite his age, he gained quite a reputation as a randy ladies man, both at the court of Louis XVI and at many of the city's finest brothels. To his wife, who had remained behind in Philadelphia, Franklin frequently wrote that he was suffering the various deprivations of France for the good of his country. He was adored by the French, who appreciated his keen wit and intelligence. The National Assembly honored Franklin with three days of mourning upon his death in 1790.

In the 18th century, progressive French officials believed that government and society should support a level of professional prostitution that might function as a transparent public institution beneficial to the security of the family. They theorized that publicly supported prostitution was preferable to the practice of each Frenchman keeping his own secret mistress. Naturally, this modern advance in social engineering was a miserable failure since Frenchmen patronized the prostitutes "and" kept their mistresses.

Napoleon III and the *Grande Horizontales*... The Second Empire (1851–1870) was a period of extraordinary excess and state-regulated prostitution continued to flourish. During the Paris International Exhibition of 1867 (the World's Fair), the brothels attracted as many tourists as the Exhibition itself. Travelers returning home observed that Paris was the most beautiful and also the most immoral city in the world.

Mid-nineteenth century Paris gave birth to the age of the *Grandes Horizontales* (the term is self-explanatory), an unprecedented social phenomenon that saw a select number of exceptionally beautiful, highly intelligent and strong-willed women rise to the very summit of wealth, power and influence.

These ambitious women amassed great fortunes while serving as the mistresses of Emperor Napoleon III, his ministers and the members of his court. They were relentlessly pursued and indulged by the wealthy industrialists of their age, who often ruined themselves financially in an effort to win their favor. The *Grandes Horizontales* were an indispensable part social life in the capital and they became the gilded super stars of their era. The most celebrated were Leonide LeBlanc (mistress of both Napoleon III and Prime Minister Georges Clemenceau), Apollonie Sabatier (nicknamed *La Présidente*), Marquise de Paiva *(La Paiva)* and the Comtesse de Castiglione. And finally, there was the poignant and tragic Alphonsine Duplessis, who, following her early death, was immortalized in the romantic novel and play *Lady of the Camellias (La Dame aux Camélias)* by Alexandre Dumas fils (one of her lovers) and later by Verdi's opera *La Traviata.*

La Belle Époque... During *La Belle Époque,* as the years between 1880 and 1914 came to be known, Paris emerged as the global center of art, fashion and literature, but even more, it transformed itself into the elegant and undisputed "world capital of pleasure."

Long before the motion picture emerged as the dominant public media and film stars became the great media focus, the opera theater and ballet were home to the stars of their day. In Paris aristocrats and the wealthy flocked to the *Opera Garnier* to see the splendid women of the stage, who could easily be taken as a mistress.

During this same period, a new form of entertainment appeared in the guise of the risqué cabaret show. The most famous cabaret of the period was the *Moulin Rouge* (opened in October 1889) in Montmartre. The district became the center of an energetic nightlife featuring dance halls, cabarets and cafés filled with the *bourgeois* in search of wanton pleasure.

The Grand Bordellos *(Maisons Closes)*... During the period of 1870 to 1947, Paris established some of the most opulent and palatial bordellos ever seen in history. These venerable establishments were patronized by royalty, movie stars, government ministers, wealthy merchants and fine society gentlemen from every nation.

The *maisons closes* (closed houses) were state-licensed brothels where prostitutes had regular medical exams and worked in a highly regulated environment. In the early 1900s as many as 180 such establishments existed in Paris with more than 100,000 prostitutes practicing their trade.

Universally celebrated as the most luxurious bordello of the late 19th and early 20th century, Le Chabanais was so named due to its address at 12 rue Chabanais, a small side street near the Louvre. A wealthy member of Parisian high society named Madame Kelly opened the establishment in 1878 and it proceeded to earn a brilliant reputation. Among Le Chabanais' better known patrons were the Prince of Wales, later King Edward VII (who maintained a permanent suite), King Leopold of Belgium, Cary Grant, Charlie Chaplin, Humphrey Bogart, Katherine Hepburn, Fatty Arbuckle, Eric von Stroheim, Salvador Dali, Marlene Dietrich (who snuck in dressed as a man) and the ever lusty Mae West.

"Bertie," the Prince of Wales (Queen Victoria's oldest son) was known to particularly enjoy Champagne baths with a couple of female companions, taken in a giant copper tub shaped like a swan. He even had a kinky apparatus built to suit his amorous needs, a kind of love-seat *(siege d'amour)* with various straps and stirrups. Unfortunately this was a necessity because the Prince was terribly overweight and was forced to make love standing up.

The prince had a lascivious tempermant and a naughty sense of humor. While attending an elegant Parisian social event he was introduced to the renowned, high-class courtesan Guila Barucci. For his own amusement he requested that she immediately remove her gown and she submissively complied to the shock of the other guests.

The seven floors of Le Chabanais were sumptuously decorated, offering guests a choice of many exotic suites, each decorated with a different theme. There was the exotic Hindu Suite, the French style Louis XIV Suite and the famous Japanese Suite, which had won the prize for best design at the Paris Universal Exhibition of 1900. At the end of the Exhibition, the pavilion was disassembled then reassembled at Le Chabanais.

A wardrobe of imaginative and exotic costumes was kept by the house so the beautiful hostesses could dress appropriately to meet the whim of their customers. Popular wardrobe selections included a wedding dress, nun's habit and the outfit of an innocent milkmaid.

The house was open by "appointment only" in order to discreetly protect the royal and famous patrons. The salons were resplendent with erotic murals painted by Toulouse-Lautrec, another permanent resident of the house, who while famously short in stature was otherwise well-endowed. He often quipped "I may only be a small coffee-pot but I have a big spout." Other amenities included several, elegant bars, a gourmet restaurant and a lively cabaret show.

Other swanky establishments included La One Two Two located at 122 rue de Provence, near the St-Lazare train station and Le Sphinx on blvd Edgar-Quinet.

La One Two Two provided customers with their own outrageous selection of fantasy inspired salons, including: a nautical suite made-up as the mahogany-paneled cabin of a trans-Atlantic ocean liner; a marble Greek temple and a chilly Artic Igloo. Certainly the most innovative backdrop for a randy tryst was the luxurious Orient Express–style sleeping compartment featuring a moving landscape behind a mock window and the recorded clickety-clack of train rails.

In the house's fabled restaurant, *Boeuf à la Ficelle,* waitresses clad in "only" high heels and a small, white apron served imported Iranian caviar, vintage bottles of Bollinger Champagne and expertly prepared haute cuisine.

The other highly celebrated Parisian bordello was Le Sphinx on blvd Edgar-Quinet. Opened in 1931 with an Egyptian theme, its suites were named after famous French personalities. Le Sphinx was favored by American actors Clark Gable, Gary Cooper, Errol Flynn and John Barrymore as well as writer and sensualist Henry Miller.

French author Marcel Proust was a devotee of the *maisons closes* but spurned the tender services of the house. He much preferred to observe others through a hole drilled in the floor of his bed chamber.

These institutions were much more than lavish brothels, they were more akin to an exclusive private club where the rich and famous could gather among their peers to relax, socialize and carouse. Parisians of the era were justly proud that their city offered the most illustrious houses of intrigue and dissipation in the world.

But after the horrors of the war and occupation, a Socialist-leaning French Parliament passed the Marthe Richard law in 1946, shutting down all of the *maisons closes* but permitting prostitutes to continue working individually. On May 8, 1951, the luxurious furnishings of Le Chabanais were put up for public auction. Edward VII's notorious swan-shaped bathtub sold for 110,000 francs and later ended up in the home of artist Salvador Dali. It was the end of an era.

In 1963 Hollywood saluted the Paris prostitute in Billy Wilder's zany comedy *Irma La Douce,* about a police officer (Jack Lemmon) who gets fired, becomes a pimp, falls in love and eventually marries his favorite working girl Shirley MacLaine.

The Debate Continues... Since the day in 1946 that the *maisons closes* were shut down, a debate has raged among the French regarding the morality of prostitution in contemporary society.

In 2003 as part of a general crack-down on crime, the French government passed a series of new laws outlawing public soliciting. While prostitution remained legal, the new approach sought to prosecute anyone "actively or passively" soliciting sex by means of their "dress or posture." In short, the authorities would no longer tolerate the traditional "Irma la Douce" style prostitute standing under a street lamp, wearing fish-net stockings and a come-hither look. The new laws had no direct legal implications for customers.

The campaign was designed to improve the image of Paris by forcing the streetwalker off the street and to a large extent it was successful. Most working girls disappeared from the central boulevards and decamped to the suburbs. An unintended consequence has been a marked increase in the number of call girls and escort services. This appears to be acceptable to the government since the practice is out of the public eye. Prostitution is still legal in France, but only if one practices as an individual and is not an employee of another person or entity. The government's argument is that if one is self-employed she or he is not being exploited.

While there is nothing romantic or charming about prostitution, the ladies of the night and the seedy side of Paris were, and still are part of the city's lore. The French, who pride themselves on their tolerance, remain quite conflicted on this issue. Center-right Parliamentarian Françoise de Panafieu re-ignited the debate when she suggested that the matter could best be resolved by reintroducing state-controlled brothels similar to those operating in Germany and Holland. Certain factions hope to see prostitutes qualify for state social security and pension benefits, while others condemn all forms of prostitution as exploitation and want to see it totally abolished. A poll taken shortly after the new 2003 law went into effect revealed that nearly two-thirds of the population favored reopening the luxurious old maisons closes.

The Historic Red Light Districts of Paris... The two historic red light districts of Paris *(place Pigalle* and *rue St-Denis)* have been in existence for centuries. While they remain popular with tourists, streetwalkers are now absent from the street.

Visiting the Old Red Light Districts... Over time, the city's infamous red light districts evolved into erotic entertainment areas where tourists visit cabaret shows, strip clubs and other adult amusements. Some of the major tour agencies (see Paris Vision and Grey-Line) offer "Naughty Paris" guided tours that usually include one of the major cabarets.

Pigalle—Red Light District—9th & 18th Arr. Métro: Pigalle... Montmartre is one of Paris's most historic and colorful districts, dominated by the Romano-Byzantine style Basilica de Sacre-Coeur at the top of Butte Montmartre. It is also home to the famous artist's haven Place du Tertre. On a clear day, the views over the city from Sacre-Coeur are stunning. In the past the neighborhood was home to many of the city's most celebrated artists including Renoir, Van Gogh, Picasso, Toulouse-Lautrec, Matisse and Degas. In fact place Pigalle is named after Jean-Baptiste Pigalle, a neoclassical sculptor whose works are on display in the Louvre.

Place Pigalle, on the border of the 9th and 18th Arrondissements, was popular with the soldiers of every war since the Franco-Prussian War of 1870. It was frequented by American soldiers in World War I, German soldiers during the Occupation, and American and allied soldiers following the 1944 liberation.

In recent years trendy rock and jazz clubs have appeared among the numerous hostess bars, erotic theaters and sex shops. Pigalle is an area where respectability and sleaze rub shoulders. The area is also home to the Moulin Rouge and the *Musée d'Erotisme* (Erotic Museum).

St-Denis—Red Light District—2nd Arr. Métro: Reamur Sebastopol... St-Denis is located in the heart of Paris near Les Halles and the Pompidou Center. Rue St-Denis was the original Roman road leading out of the city to the north. For 800 years, *Les Halles* (the halls), established in 1183, served as the city's primary marketplace for foodstuffs (and prostitution flourished in the area). It was the location where Jack Lemmon toiled away carrying sides of beef in *Irma La Douce*. Émile Zola referred to the market as *le ventre de Paris,* (the belly of Paris). Despite the rabid opposition of preservationists, mindless local politicians approved the destruction of the magnificant cast-iron and glass pavilions in 1971. The elegant structures built in the Napoleonic era were replaced by a soulless, underground shopping mall *(Forum des Halles).*

Chapter Fifteen:
Sexy French Glossary & Phrasebook

Chapter Fifteen:

"The French language is a woman. And this woman is so beautiful, so proud, so modest, so tough, so touching, so voluptuous, so chaste, so noble, so familiar, so crazy, so wise that one loves her with all one's soul, and one is never tempted to be unfaithful to her."

~ Anatole France ~

The glossary and phrasebook are designed to assist you in various social situations: meeting, flirting, dating and sexual play. And for good measure, we have added a few choice French insults and a bit of vulgar, salacious slang.

English	**French** French Pronunciation
(M) = masculine form (F) =	feminine form
Greetings & Introductions	
Good day	Bonjour (add Monsieur or Madame) bon-zhoor
Good evening	Bon soir bon-swar
Hello & goodbye	Salut sah-loo
How are you?	Comment allez-vous? (formal) ko-mohn tah-lay voo
Fine, and you?	Très bien, et vous? treh bee-ehn, ay voo?
How's it going?	Ça va? (informal) sa vah? A brief and casual greeting—you may also answer by saying "ca va."
Good-by	Au revoir oh ruh-vwar
See you soon	A bientot ah be-en-tow
Have a nice day	Bonne journee bohn zhur nay
I'd like to introduce ___	Je vous présente jeuh vu pray-zhant
What is your name?	Comment vous appellez-vous? kom-mohn voo-za-peh-lay voo
My name is___	Je m'appelle___ jeuh mah-pell
Sorry, I don't speak French	Désolé, je ne parle pas français day-zo-lay zhuh nuh parhle pah frahn-say

Common Courtesy

Mr	Monsieur (abbreviated as: M.) muh-syuh
Madam/Mrs/Ms	Madame (abbreviated as: Mme) ma-dam
Miss	Mademoiselle (young woman) (abbreviated as: Mlle) mad-mwa-zelle
Thank you	Merci (madame/monsieur) mair-see (mah-dahm/miss-your)
Thanks, that's very kind	Merci, c'est gentil mare-see say jhon-tee
I'm sorry	Desolé day-zoh-lay
Yes	Oui Wee
No	Non Nohn
Agreed (or OK)	D'accord dah-core
Please	S'il vous plait seel voo play
Here	Ici ee-see
That's ok	De rien dah ree-ehn
Excuse me/sorry	Excusez-moi ex-koo-zay mwah
Pardon me (in a crowd)	Pardonnez-moi pahr-dohn-eh mwah
Right, so, or well	Bon! bohn

Everyday Conversation

Do you speak English?	Parlez-vous anglais? par-lay voo zohn-glay
I speak a little French	Je parle un peu de français jeuh parl-unh puh duh frahn-say
I don't speak French	Je ne parle pas français. jeuh nuh parl pah frahn-say
Can you help me?	Est-ce que vous pouvez m'aider? Ess kuh voo poovay may-day

I have a question	J'ai une question zhay oone kes-ch uhn
I don't understand	Je ne comprends pas. zhuh nuh kohm-prah-n pah
Pleased to meet you	Enchanté(e) ah-nn-shahn-tay
Please speak slowly	Parlez lentement par-lay lehn-ta-mohn
I don't know	Je ne sais pas. zhuh-nuh say pah
The check, please	L'addition, s'il vous plait la-dis-see ohn, see-voo-play

Flirtation & Seduction

What's your name?	Comment vous appelez-vous? koh-maw n voo zah-play voo
My name is ____	Je m'appelle ____ zhuh ma-pell
Are you French?	Êtes-vous français? (M) / française (F)? eht voo frahn-say/fran-sez
I'm English/American	Je suis anglais(e)/américain(e). zhuh swee ehn-glay/ah mehr ree kehn
Where do you live?	Où habitez-vous? ooh ah-bee-tay voo
I live in London/New York	J'habite à Londres/New York zhah-beet a lown-druh/New York
How old are you?	Quel âge avez-vous? kell ah zhay- voo
I'm ___ years old	J'ai ___ ans. zhay ___ ahhn
Are you married?	Etes-vous marié? (M)/mariée (F)? Eht voo mar-yay?
I'm single	Je suis célibataire. jeuh swee cell-ahh-buh-tehr
I'm married	Je suis marié(e). jeuh swee mar-yay
I'm divorced	Je suis divorcé(e). jeuh swee duh vor-say
Want to dance?	Voulez danser? voo-lay dahn-say
You are very sweet	Vous êtes très gentil (M)/gentile (F). voo zet tray zhan-tee/jhan-teel

You are very beautiful	Vous êtes très beau. voo zeht tray bow
Will you come with me to a café?	Voulez-vous venir avec moi dans un café? voo-lay voo don-nay ah-vehk mwah dahn zuhn caf-fay
Please give me your phone number?	Veuillez me donner votre numéro de telephone? voo-lay muh don-nay vote-truh noom-air-oh duh tel eh phohn
Do you have a business card?	Avez-vous une carte de visite? Ah-vay voo oohn kart duh viz-eet
Will you go to dinner with me?	Volonté vous allez au resto avec moi? vo-lahn-tay voo ah-ley rest-oh ah-vek muah
How about a drink at my place?	Volonté vous avez une boisson à chez moi? vo-lahn-tay voo sah-vay oone bwah-sohn ah shay mwah?
Where do you live in Paris?	Où habitez-vous a Paris? ooh ah-beh-tay voo ahh Pah-ree?
I'm at the ____Hotel	Je suis a l'hotel ____ zhuh swee ah loh-tel ____
I have an apartment at ____	J'ai un appartement a ____ jhay unh apar-mehnt ah ____
You are so sexy!	Tu es si sexy! too eh see sek-see
I'm hot	Il fait chaud. Il fay show

In French when you feel that the "temperature" is *hot,* you say *Il fait chaud.* However, avoid saying *Je suis chaud* to the guy standing next to you on the Métro as it means "I am hot for sex."

I'm hot	Je suis chaud. zhuh swee show

I'm hot for sex! You are perfectly free to say this to the guy standing next to you on the Métro if you don't care about the stupid weather and are looking for a good time.

My darling	Ma cheri / mon cher mah share-ree / mohn share
My darling	Ma biche (means literally "my doe") mah beesh

I love you — Je t'aime
zhuh tehm

I adore you — Je t'adore
zhuh tah-door

I want to go to bed with you — Je voudrais coucher avec toi
zhuh voo-dray koo-shay ah-vek too-ah

Sex Play

To have an affair — Avoir une aventure
Ah-vwh-are oohn ah-ven-choor

Let's go to the bedroom — Allons à la chambre à coucher
ah lohn ah lah sha bruh ah coo shay

You have a beautiful body — Tu as un très beau corps
too ah unh tray bow core

Kiss me — Embrasse-moi
ehm-bra suh mwah

A Kiss (noun) — Un baiser
unh bay-zay
(don't confuse this with the verb)

To fuck (verb) — Baiser
bay-zay

Take your clothes off — Déshabille-toi.
deh-shah-be twah

Your lingerie is very sexy — Votre lingerie est trés sexy.
vo-truh lahn-gher-ay ay tray sek-see

I love cunnilingus — J'aime *lecher la chatte* (lick the cat).
zhehm lesh-eh la shat

Tickle me — Chatouille-moi.
cha-too-ee muah

Do you have condoms? — Avez-vous des capotes?
ah-veh voo day kah-powt

A condom is also referred to as a *preservatif.* Avoid asking the waiter if there are preservatifs in your food as he will only think you are another of those very bizarre Américains!

I want to fuck you — Je veux te prendre.
zhuh vou-tuh prahn-druh

Was it good for you? — C'etait bon?
Set-tay bohn?
Best said while lighting a Gauloise!

Do it again! — On recommence!
ohn re-koh-mahnse

Best said after waiting the requisite amount of time, depending upon the man's age

Spank me!	Donne-moi une fessee! donny mwah oone fess-ay
This is unbelievable!	C'est incroyable! say tahn kroy ahh bluh
I like it	Ça me plait sah muh play
I don't like it	Ça ne me plaît pas. sah nuh muh play pah
Leave me alone!	Laissez-moi tranquille! lay-say mwah trahn-keel

Terminology

Boyfriend — Copain
koh-paah

Girlfriend — Copine
ko-peen

Coquette — Coquette
ko-kette

Female who makes teasing sexual or romantic overtures; a flirt

Husband — Un mari
unh mah-ree

Wife — Une femme
oone feh-muh

Mistress — Maîtresse
may-trehss

Lover — Un amant (M) / Une amante (F)
unh ah-mah / oone ah-mahnt

Overnight Bag — Baise-en-ville
bays-ahn-vee

Means literally "screw in town" – thus the small bag carried by someone visiting their lover

To flirt — Flirter
fler-tehr

Love at first sight — Le coup-de-foudre
le coo duh foo-druh
Literally means "the bolt of lightning"

Buns, bottom, ass — Fesse
fess

Menstruation — Les Anglais
layz ahn-glay

French slang for the "Redcoats have landed," meaning menstruation has begun. This is just one of a thousand ways that the French manage to get a little dig in at the Brits.

Condom	Preservatif or capote pruh-sehr-vah-tif, kah-poat

What the Brits refer to as a *French letter.* Just one of a thousand ways the Brits get a little dig in at the French.

Sexual Orgasm	Petit mort peh-tee more Literally translates as "the little death"
Female climax	L'extase lex-tah-zz
Vibrator	Vibromasseur vi-bro-mass-oor
Dildo	Godemichet go-duh-me-shay
Orgy	Partouze par-tooz
Toilet, water closet	WC doob-ya say
Caca	Ca ca ka ka

Those squishy, brown gifts that one frequently encounters on the sidewalks compliments of the dogs of Paris and their blithely, oblivious owners. Parisians generally prefer those snippy, highly groomed, miniature "ankle-biters" as opposed to the "real dogs" that Americans and Brits have back home. But *vive le difference* and watch your step.

Englishman (Brit)	Rosbif rohss-biff

French slang - a fairly inoffensive insult that the French have used for the Brits since the 18th century. Relates to the English style of cooking beef.

Frog (a Frenchman)	Grenouille grahn-wee

English slang - a fairly inoffensive insult used by the Brits to refer to the French. The term has been in use since the 13th century. It originally applied to Jesuits, those "Papists" across the Channel, but evolved to mean all Frenchmen. It may also refer to a favored item on most French menus.

Parisian	Parisien (M) / Parisienne (F) pah-ree-see-ehn

Those wonderfully, bright, witty, and sophisticated residents of Paris, who very much like New Yorkers, are widely recognized (particularly among themselves) to be far superior to all those hopeless, uncultured peasants, rubes and twits from anywhere else (i.e., the provinces).

The provinces — Les provinces
lay prah-VAHN-ss

The pastoral home of the good-natured inhabitants of *La France profonde* (deep France). To suggest that *provincials* have little affection for their countrymen in the capital would be a monumental understatement.

The Americans — Les Américains
lez ay-mehr-ee-cahn

Those happy-go-lucky folks from the other side of the Atlantic who exported *le jazz, le Big Mac* and *le cowboy* to the world. They adore French cuisine, Champagne, and French women.

The French — Les Français
lay frahn-say

The idiosyncratic, but lovable race residing in the land of the Gauls. *Les Américains* never seem to tire of bringing up the fact that they had to save *Les Frogs* in both WWI and WWII. But *Les Frogs* like to remind them that Louis XVI had to send the powerful French Navy and millions in financial aide to save them during the Revolution of 1776. Otherwise, the Yanks might still be a colony of *Les Rosbifs.* The French adore American movies and pop culture.

Salacious Slang

The degree to which one uses street slang in France depends upon your age, peer group and the social setting. Be judicious and remember, when you're not fluent in a foreign language, you may come off sounding a lot like Borat.

Shit! — Merde!
mehr-d

The very broadly utilized, all-purpose French epithet

Guy, dude, man — Mec
mek

Girl, woman — Gonzesse
gohn-zesse

Mistress — Nana
nah-nah

Breasts, tits — Tetons
teytohns

Penis	Bite beet
Female genitalia	Chatte (literally means the cat) shat
Ass, buns, bum	Cul kull
Clitoris	Clito kli-toe
To fuck	Baiser (verb) bey-say
Blowjob	Pipe peep
Smoke the cigar	Fumer le cigare foo-MAY luh sig-ARH to give a guy oral sex (as in Monica L.)
To come	Jouir (a verb literally meaning "to rejoice") joo-eh
Threesome	Ménage a trois may-nahh-juh-twah
To perform cunnilingus	Brouter le cresson bru-tay luh cress-onh

This literally translates: "to graze the watercress"

Withering Insults

Bastard	Salud sal-lo
Bitch	Salope sa-lop
Idiot, moron (male)	Con ko
Idiot, moron (female)	Conne kohn
Easy lay	Paillasson paa-ah-sohn
Oaf, fool (M)	Beauf booff
Silly girl, twit	Bécasse bey-kaas
Cuckold	Cocu ko-coo
Whore	Pute, putain poot, poot-ahn

Dickhead	Tête de noeud tet dan-ner
You are a stupid imbecile	Vous êtes un imbécile stupide vooz-et unh em-beh-ceel stu-peed
Mind your own business!	T'occupe! toc-yoop
Fuck off!	Fous le camps! foo luh cahhn
Fuck you!!	Va te faire foutre! vah-tuh fair foo-tr-uh
You've put on weight	Tu as grossi tu ah gro-see

For any French woman who compulsively strives to remain thin, this is the ultimate insult.

INDEX

A l'Enseigne des Oudin, 109
Acanthus Paris, 120
Alice Cadolle, 45
Amnesia Café, 128
Angélina, 76
Anne Sémonin Spa, 93
Au Bonheur du Jour, 109
Au Lapin Agile, 90
Au Plurial Club, 123
Au Printemps, 46
Autour de Christophe Robin, 94
Aviation Club de France, 103
Banana Café, 128
Bar du Hotel Costes, 80
Bars & Lounges, 78
Batofar, 83
Berluti Shoes, 52
Biking, 98
Black Calvados (BC), 77
bobos, 113
Buddha Bar, 78
Cabarets, 89
Casino Barriére d'Enghein-les-Bains, 103
Casinos, 102
Caves le Chapelais, 133
Chantal Thomass, 45
Chez Michou, 90
Chez Omar, 107
Chocolat Chaud, 75
chocolate, 75
Chris & Manu, 122
Christian Louboutin, 51
Cindessa de Dia, 13
Cinema, 99
cinq à sept, 37
Cinq Mondes, 91
Cithéa, 83
Classical Concerts, 106
Club Le Baron, 85
Colette, 52
Coquetry, 25
Corniola, Véronique J., 101
Courtesans, 140
Crazy Horse Saloon, 90
Crochard, Marie-Elisabeth, 106
Curiosa, 108
Dance Clubs, 82
Daniela in Love, 46
Dating, 21-26
Debra Ollivier, 17, 18, 24, 30
de l'Enclos, Ninon, 140
de Medici, Catherine, 50
de Sade, Marquis, 132
Delacroix, Eugène, 18
Dèmonia, 136
Dessous: Lingerie as Erotic Weapon, 49
Diversions, 96
Duc des Lombards, 87
Edith Wharton, 19
Edward Flaherty, 98
Ernest Chausseur, 49
Ernest Hemingway, 80
Erotic Bookstores, 109
Erotic Clubbing,116
Erotica,102, 106, 107, 116
Etiquette, 34
Fetish, 133
Fetish Culture, 133
Fetish in Paris, 138
Fetish Shopping, 136
Field Colin, 80
Fifi Chachnil, 45
Flèche d'Or, 84
Folies Bergeres, 89
François Mitterrand, 39
French Lingerie, 41
FrenchFriendFinder, 29
FUSAC, 30
Gay, 129
Gay & Lesbian Paris, 128
Gilles Néret, 40, 44, 48, 49
Glossary & Phrasebook, 147

Golden Age of Salons, 18
Grande Horizontales, 141
Hair & Beauty, 94
Harry's New York Bar, 78
Haynes, Jim, 102
Helena Frith Powell, 19, 24, 33
High Heel, 51
High Heel Shoe, 50
Hot Chocolate, 75
Hotel Britannique, 58
Hôtel des Grandes Ecoles, 60
Hôtel Le Bristol, 59
Hotel Louis II, 61
Hotel Meurice Day Spa, 93
Hotel Plaza Athénée, 81
Hotel Ritz, 80
Hotels, 60
Infidelity, 34
Intimate Cabarets, 90
Irma la Douce, 144
Jazz Clubs, 87
Jean-Paul Hévin, 74
Jim Haynes Soiree, 102
John Nollet, 95
Jonathan LeBlanc Roberts, 5
Julia Child, 103, 110
Kippen, Cameron, 50
Kong, 82
l'Ecluse, 88
L'Etoile, 83-85
L'Hôtel, 56
La Belle Époque, 108
La Brasserie Bofinger, 108
La Champmeslé, 128
La Coupole, 85
La Maison Blanche, 86
La Maison du Chocolat, 75
La Mezzanine de l'Alcazar, 79
La Milliardaire, 86
La Musardine, 109
La Nuit Dèmonia, 137
La One Two Two, 144
Ladurée, 75
Lancôme Institut, 93
Leeds, Adrian, 106
Le 32 Montorgueil Spa Nuxe, 94
Le Bar à Chocolat, 76
Le Bar du Plaza Athénée, 81
Le Bon Marché, 47
Le Cab (Cabaret), 84
Le Chabanais, 142
Le Club 2+2, 122
Le Cordon Bleu Paris, 106
Le Depot, 129
Le Dokhan's—Champagne Bar, 79
Le Fumoir, 78
Le Moulin Rouge, 89
Le Nautilus, 122
Le Paradis Latin, 90
Le Paris Paris, 84
Le Pulp, 129
Le Raidd, 129
Le Relais Saint Germain, 58
Le Ritz Club, 86
Le Rosebud, 79
Le Slow Club, 87
Le Sphinx, 143
Le Sunset, 87
Le Triptyque, 83
Le Tropic Café, 128
Le VIP, 86
Le Wagg (Club), 125
Léonide LeBlanc, 140
Les Bains Douche, 84
Les Bains du Marais, 94
Les Chandelles, 120
Les Galeries Lafayette, 46
Lesbian, 128
Libertine Clubs, 116
Librarie de l'Avenue Henri-Veyrier, 109
Librarie-Galerie Les Larmes d'Éros, 108
Lido de Paris, 89
Lingerie Shopping, 45
Luxembourg Gardens, 12, 61, 108
maître d', 28
Maria Luisa, 51
Marivaux, Pierre, 14, 15
Massage Café, 94
Maxim Nights, 86
Maxim's Restaurant, 86
Meetic, 30
Michel Perry, 51
Mix Club, 82
Musee Jacquemart André, 104
Musée Rodin, 104
Museum of Erotic Art, 104
Museum of the Romantic Life, 105
Museums, 104
Mystique, 18, 26
Nicolas Sarkozy, 18

Nightclubs, 89
Nightlife, 76
No Comment Club, 121
No Stress Café, 94
Nouveau Casino, 82
Nuit Élastique, 137
Ollivier, Debra, 19, 20, 26, 32
Open Café, 128
Overside, 121
Parc de Bagatelle, 106
Paris as Therapy, 112
Paris Plage, 99
Paris Roller, 103
Parler-Parlor, 106
Pavilion de la Reine, 60
Petit Bateau, 47
Petite Coquette, 47
Phylea, 136
Pink Paradise, 124
Place Furstenberg, 107
Place Vendôme, 53
Price, Robert, 103
Prince of Wales, 142
Princesse Tam-Tam, 45
Quai 17, 123
Quickie Massage, 94
Red Light Districts, 145
Regines, 125
Relais-Hôtel du Vieux, 61
Retro dancing, 85
Rex Club, 83
Rollerbladers, 103
Romance, 12, 13
Rykiel Woman, 52
Sabbia Rosa, 45
Saint James Paris, 61
Salacious Slang, 155
School of Seduction, 101
Secret Dessous, 46
Seduction, 13-14, 17, 21, 24
Segolene Royal, 20
Sergio Rossi, 51
Sex & Sexuality, 31
Sex Scandal, 39
Sex Toys, 52, 53
Sexuality, 31
Shopping, 42-53, 146
Soirées, 86
Sojourn in Paris, 112
Spa at Royal Monceau, 93
Spa—Four Seasons Hotel—
Georges V, 92
Spas, 92
Stilettos, 51
Stringfellow's, 124
Strip just for the Ladies, 125
Strip Tease Clubs, 124
Table Manners, 21, 26
Taverne Heni IV, 88
The Bar Hemingway, 80
Theatrhall, 136
Thigh-high boots, 51
Toulouse-Lautrec, Henri de, 142
Tuileries, 12
Uber-Chic Clubs, 85
UNICIS Paris, 30
Venal Pleasures, 140
Vicomte de Valmont, 21
Victoria Palace Hotel, 57
VIP Soirées, 86
Willi's Wine Bar, 87
Wine Bars, 87
Withering Insults, 156
Yoba La Boutique, 53

Appendix A: Paris Geographic Terminology

Left Bank *(Rive Gauche)*—The Left Bank is the portion of the city on the south side of the River Seine, which divides Paris in half. Over time, the term Left Bank has come to represent more than just a geographical section of the city; it refers to a certain lifestyle embodied in the people who reside in St-Germain-des-Prés, the Latin Quarter and Montparnasse.

Right Bank *(Rive Droite)*—The Right Bank is the portion of the city on the north side of the River Seine. The northern half of the city is known for its elegance and sophistication. Many of the city's luxury hotels, leading entertainment venues and upmarket designer shops are located on the Right Bank.

Arrondissement- Abbreviation: Arr. – (French abbreviation: e) Paris is divided into twenty "arrondissements," or districts. These districts are distributed in a circular, clockwise pattern like a nautilus shell. The 1st to the 6th arrondissements (and part of the 7th) represent the oldest portions of the city. The 1st is in the center and the others rotate out. Throughout this guide the arrondissements are referred to as 1st or 3rd Arr. etc. In French, they are abbreviated 1e or 2e. The last two digits of a Paris postal code corresponds to the arrondissement number.

SOURCES OF QUOTATIONS

The author and publishers have made every reasonable effort to contact the copyright owners of the quotations in this book. In the few cases where they may have been unsuccessful they invite copyright holders to contact them directly.

Agacinski, Sylviane. *Parity of the Sexes,* New York, Columbia University Press, 2001

Euro RSCG Worldwide Sex Survey. *Sex, Religion and Infidelity,* New York, 2004

Hévin, Jean-Paul. www.jphevin.com

Hofstede, Dr. Geert

Gallup World Poll, 2007

Kippen, Cameron, Lecturer and Shoe Historian, Curtin University of Technology, Perth, Australia, l'Institut Français d'Opinion Publique (Ifop), Paris, 2006

Néret, Gilles. Dessous—*Lingerie as Erotic Weapon*. London: Taschen, 2001.

Néret, Gilles. *1000 Dessous*. London, Taschen, 2001.

Ollivier, Debra. *What French Girls Know,* San Francisco: Salon.com, 2004.

Ollivier, Debra. *France vs. America: The Sex Front,* San Francisco: Salon.com, 2003.

Powell, Helena Frith. *Two Lipsticks and a Lover,* Gibson Square Books, London, 2006

Ikavalko, Ilkka J., *St-Sulpice*. Houston: Studios St-Sulpice, www.geocities.com/saint-sulpice,1994-2003

TNS-Sofres Poll

www.insenses.org

www.yobaparis.com

CPSIA information can be obtained at www.ICGtesting.com
Printed in the USA
240715LV00006B/12/P